Produced by Copyright Studio, Paris
Editor : Jean-Paul Paireault
Cooking Editor : Catherine Monnet
Art Director : Jacques Hennaux
Design : Sandrine Desbordes

MALLARD PRESS

An imprint of BDD Promotional Book Company, Inc.,
666 Fifth Avenue, New York, N.Y. 10103
Mallard Press and its accompanying design and logo
are trademarks of BDD Promotional Book Company, Inc.

CLB 2373
© 1990 Colour Library Books Ltd., Godalming, Surrey, England.
Color separations by Hong Kong Graphic Arts Ltd., Hong Kong.
Printed and bound in Hong Kong by Leefung Asco Printers Ltd.
All rights reserved.
ISBN 0 792 45229 1

THE ART
O F
COOKING

MALLARD
PRESS

CONTENTS

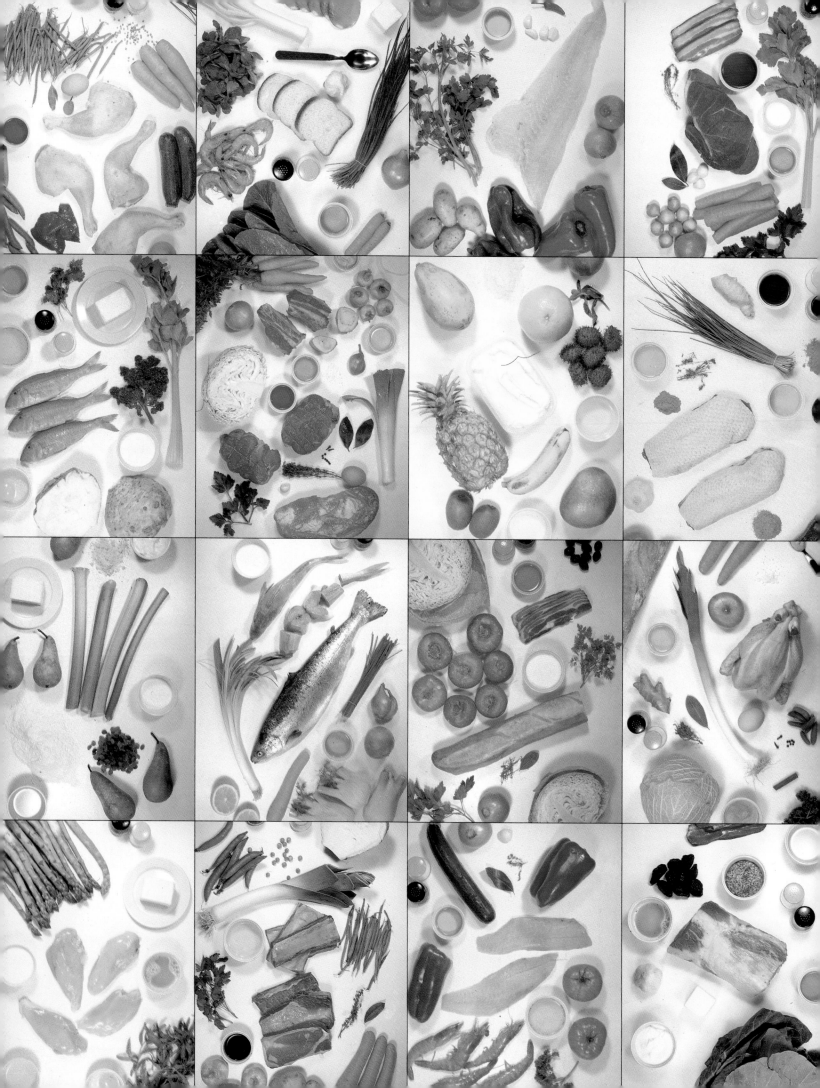

INTRODUCTION

The title of this cookery book gives more than just a clue as to its contents, but it still tells only half the story. The recipes included here are indeed all about the style and art of modern cooking, but they are not about complicated preparation or cooking techniques. Just the opposite. These recipes are about helping you to produce, simply and without fuss, in your own kitchen, the type of dishes seen in today's more fashionable restaurants. Dishes which, with their emphasis on increasingly artful and elegant presentation, often look dauntingly difficult to reproduce.

This book, however, enables you to do just that by presenting each recipe with explicit instructions in an illustrated, step-by-step format, including, wherever it might be useful, specific preparation techniques. The necessary ingredients and utensils are carefully listed at the beginning of each recipe and, to stimulate your taste buds, the recipes are preceded by a beautiful color photograph of the finished dish, together with a detailed description of the dish itself. Furthermore, each recipe has been tested and retested by its originator, French chef Frédéric Lebain, to make it as easy as possible for you to obtain the same perfect results as he has.

The recipes have, of course, been developed with the everyday cook in mind, but occasionally they include special ingredients which may be more difficult to find. In this case, alternative ingredients are always suggested.

So, whether it's simply for a family meal or for an elegant dinner party, bring a little restaurant glamour into your home with The Art of Cooking.

BASIL

Fresh basil is one of the best herbs to add to tomato or egg dishes. The leaves, can also be used whole in green salads, or chopped and added to a vinaigrette. Use it to flavor butter or with bland fish.

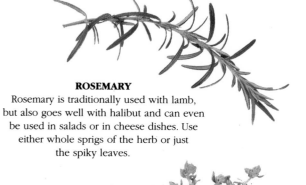

ROSEMARY

Rosemary is traditionally used with lamb, but also goes well with halibut and can even be used in salads or in cheese dishes. Use either whole sprigs of the herb or just the spiky leaves.

THE HERBS

Fresh herbs not only add flavor to but improve the appearance of any gourmet dish. Certain herbs marry well with particular foods but there are no hard and fast rules. A keen cook can experiment to create original and tasty combinations.

THYME

Thyme is best known as an ingredient of bouquets garnis. It has a strong flavor and should be added sparingly to grilled meat or fish. Chop the fresh leaves, and add to mashed potatoes or other vegetable dishes.

DILL

Dill is particularly good in fish dishes. Try adding extra space the chopped leaves to green or raw vegetable salads. The seeds are good with cucumber, or crushed in lamb stews.

CHERVIL

Similar to parsley in appearance, it can be used in the same ways, too, although its slightly aniseed flavor means it should be used more sparingly.

PARSLEY
Curly-leaved parsley is best reserved for decoration ; use the flat-leaved variety for cooking. The leaves can be used whole, or chopped and added to salads and sauces or sprinkled over cooked vegetables.

CHIVES
Chives have a mild onion flavor which makes them a versatile seasoning for many dishes, particularly in soups, with freshwater fish and in sauces such as Béarnaise or vinaigrette.

CORIANDER
Coriander is an annual plant native to the Mediterranean region but which now grows wild in most parts of Europe. It is one of the oldest herbs known to man and the leaves can be used in a variety of dishes from salads to curries.

BAY
An evergreen shrub, native to Mediterranean countries, whose leaves can be used fresh, or dried, sliced, chopped or powdered to add flavor to stocks, stews and pâtés. Indispensable in bouquets garnis.

MINT
The mint plant comes originally from the Mediterranean, where it was highly esteemed in ancient times as a symbol of hospitality. Its uses are wide ranging.

SAGE
Sage is used not only in sage and onion stuffing, but also with roast pork or in beef stews. The fresh leaves, chopped, are good in salads and on tomatoes.

TARRAGON
Tarragon has a distinctive flavor ; it can be finely chopped and added to a vinaigrette. It also enhances meat, fish and chicken dishes. Chopped and added to butter it flavours bland vegetables.

LEMON GRASS
Lemon grass is a member of the mint family. The leaves have a strong, lemony scent and can be used to season a variety of savory dishes.

JUNIPER BERRIES

Juniper berries have a peppery, slightly resinous
flavor. They are best lightly crushed and added
to game dishes and marinade for raw fish.

CUMIN

An aromatic plant, the seeds
are dried and used crushed
or whole in soups and
breads, and to flavor meat
and fish dishes.

THE SPICES

Spices can transform an ordinary meal into an

adventure. Ready-ground spices rapidly lose their flavor,

so buy only small quantities at a time, store in airtight

containers and never keep them for more than a year.

NUTMEG

Although usually sold ground, nutmeg
is best bought as white kernels and freshly
grated, as required. It is commonly used
in any type of potato dish, or in
white sauces and soufflés.

CLOVES

Cloves are the dried, unopened buds of and evergreen
tree. They give a sharp, spicy flavor when added whole
to stews or marinades. When finely ground, they are
often used in association with cinnamon for desserts.

CURRY POWDER

This is a mixture of ground Asian spices, most commonly
turmeric, coriander, chili, cumin, mustard seed and
fenugreek. The different proportions of these spices
accounts for the degree of hotness of the curry powder.

CAYENNE PEPPER

The dried pods of a red chili pepper native to Central
America are ground to produce this hot spice.

CARDAMOM

Cardamom is a member of the ginger family, native to India and also
extensively cultivated in Malabar and Ceylon. Use the seeds to flavor hot fruit
punches, pickles, mulled wines, breads, biscuits and desserts.

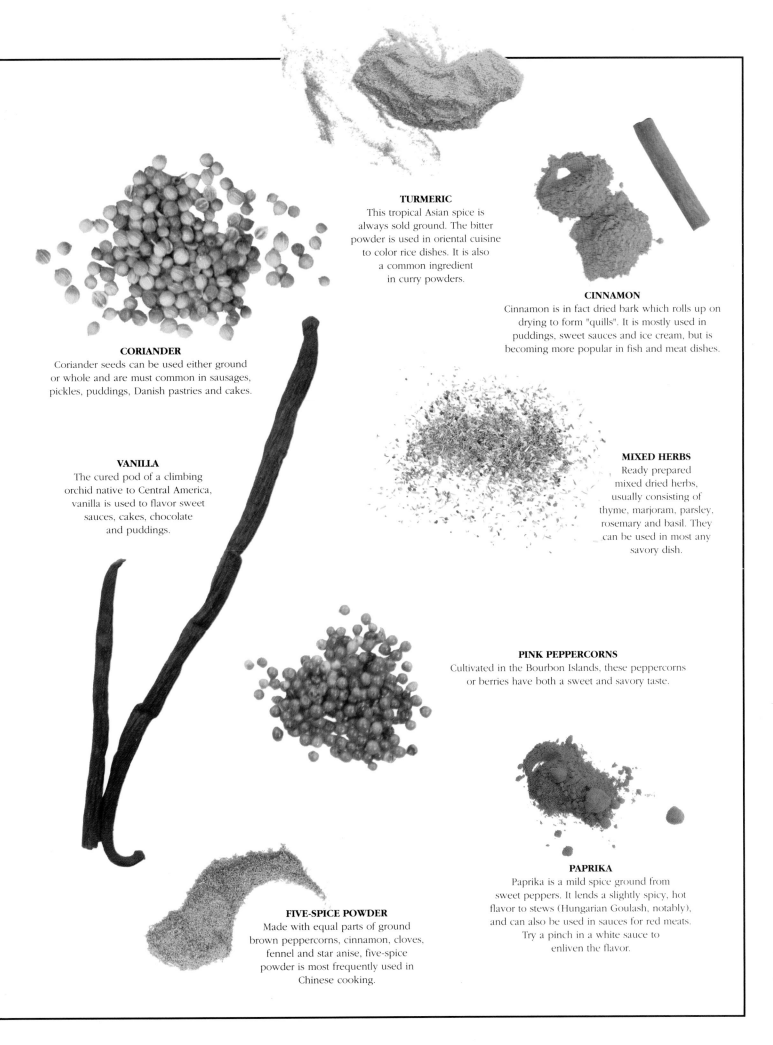

TURMERIC
This tropical Asian spice is always sold ground. The bitter powder is used in oriental cuisine to color rice dishes. It is also a common ingredient in curry powders.

CINNAMON
Cinnamon is in fact dried bark which rolls up on drying to form "quills". It is mostly used in puddings, sweet sauces and ice cream, but is becoming more popular in fish and meat dishes.

CORIANDER
Coriander seeds can be used either ground or whole and are must common in sausages, pickles, puddings, Danish pastries and cakes.

VANILLA
The cured pod of a climbing orchid native to Central America, vanilla is used to flavor sweet sauces, cakes, chocolate and puddings.

MIXED HERBS
Ready prepared mixed dried herbs, usually consisting of thyme, marjoram, parsley, rosemary and basil. They can be used in most any savory dish.

PINK PEPPERCORNS
Cultivated in the Bourbon Islands, these peppercorns or berries have both a sweet and savory taste.

PAPRIKA
Paprika is a mild spice ground from sweet peppers. It lends a slightly spicy, hot flavor to stews (Hungarian Goulash, notably), and can also be used in sauces for red meats. Try a pinch in a white sauce to enliven the flavor.

FIVE-SPICE POWDER
Made with equal parts of ground brown peppercorns, cinnamon, cloves, fennel and star anise, five-spice powder is most frequently used in Chinese cooking.

SMALL CARVING KNIFE
Equipped with a long fine, blade
for thin slicing.

NON-STICK, SAUCEPAN
Ideal for cooking
medium quantities, such as
pastas and sauces.

THE UTENSILS

A cook's utensils, like a workman's tools, can often

determine his success or failure. Well constructed pots

and pans, sharp knives and proper cooking tools, greatly

facilitate food preparation. Today we have the added

advantage of time saving machines, mixers,

processors, etc.

PASTA MACHINE
Enables you to make fresh homemade pasta.
It usually consists of a roller for flattening the dough
and an attachment for cutting pasta in to various
shapes : tagliatelle, spaghetti, etc.

GRATER
For cutting or shredding
different shapes of vegetables quickly
and evenly, such as julienne slices, etc.

MEDIUM CHOPPING KNIFE
A medium-sized knife, good for chopping vegetables and
small cuts of meat. It is also used to remove the flesh from
tomatoes or to peel fruits such as lemons.

FINE SIEVE
To strain sauces and
purées, to eliminate
impurities. It is often lined
with fine cheesecloth for
straining stocks or
liquid sauces.

VEGETABLE PEELER
Ideal for peeling most
fruits and vegetables ;
also used to remove
fish bones.

GLASS BAKING DISH
Recommended for baking, especially for
browning, as in "au gratin" dishes or spare
ribs. Very resistant to high temperatures.

RUBBER SPATULA
Ideal for transferring creams and sauces from one
container to another without waste.

LARGE NON-STICK FLAMEPROOF CASSEROLE
Used for cooking large joints of meat
or vegetables. It can also be used to sauté or
prepare dishes that require long,
slow cooking.

HEAVY-BOTTOMED SAUCEPAN
Used for bringing liquids such as milk
to a rapid boil, or for making small
quantities of sauce.

FILLETING KNIFE
Quite flexible, used mostly for
filleting any variety of fish.

LARGE NON-STICK FRYING PAN
For cooking large quantities of rice,
seafood or anything else in bulk.

LADLE
For spooning up liquids
or creams. Can be used
as a measure ; the
quantities vary with the
different models.

CLEAVER
Used for breaking up or chopping bones
or for flattening meat into scallops.

HAND-HELD ELECTRIC BLENDER
Indispensable for liquidising sauces, it has
various speeds and can be battery operated
for convenience. It is equally useful for
making fresh fruit purées or "coulis".

MIXING BOWL
With its slightly rounded base,
this is excellent for preparing
pastry dough, for making sweet
or savory sauces and also for
whipping cream or egg whites.

METAL WHISK
Used in the preparation of numerous mixtures,
sauces, creams, etc. The large wire whisk is
used to beat double cream or egg whites.

LARGE CHOPPING KNIFE
For finely chopping herbs or
vegetables, or for cutting vegetables
into various shapes.

ALL-PURPOSE KNIFE
Enables you to trim
and shape vegetables or for
any basic cutting job. Also
used for boning chicken.

CONSOMMÉ

WITH

CRUNCHY

VEGETABLES

SERVES : 6

PREPARATION TIME : 45 Minutes
COOKING TIME : 2 Hours 30 Minutes

A clear, light soup of enriched meat stock, which can be served either hot or cold. Raw, diced vegetables are added at the last minute to retain their crispness and fresh flavor.

INGREDIENTS

- [ ] 2¼lbs stewing beef (have the butcher chop the bones)
- [ ] 3 carrots
- [ ] 2 turnips
- [ ] ½lb potatoes
- [ ] 1 cup green beans
- [ ] ½ large celeriac
- [ ] 1 leek
- [ ] Bouquet garni (parsley, thyme, bay leaf)
- [ ] 1 cup peas
- [ ] 2 egg whites
- [ ] 2 tbsps soy sauce
- [ ] 2 sprigs parsley
- [ ] Salt and pepper

1 Cut off any fat on the meat; roll the beef up and tie neatly. Reserve the bones.

2 Peel the carrots and turnip. Reserve the peelings. Cut the vegetables in slices, then sticks and finally dice.

3 Make the bouquet garni by tying together the parsley, thyme and bay leaf.

4 In a casserole, cover the meat, bones and vegetable peelings with cold water and add the bouquet garni. Cook for 2 hours 30 minutes, skimming off the foam.

5
Peel the potatoes and cube them, together with the green beans. Put the potatoes in water to prevent discoloration and set aside.

9
Lightly beat the egg whites into the leeks for 5 seconds, and add to the cooled consommé. Bring to a boil, and simmer for 5 minutes, stirring constantly. Add the soy sauce and pepper.

6
Peel, trim and cube the celeriac. Wash and finely dice the leek. Shell the peas.

10
Strain the stock through a sieve lined with cheesecloth. Keep the stock warm.

7
Boil the diced vegetables separately, then the peas. Drain, rinse and set aside.

11
Wash and trim the parsley. Dry well and finely chop all the leafy parts.

8
When the meat is done, remove, slice through the string and cube half of the meat (reserve the other half for another use). Allow the stock and meat to cool.

12
Divide the vegetables and meat between 6 soup plates, pour over the hot consommé, and serve with chopped parsley.

TURNIP

AND

CABBAGE SOUP

SERVES : 6

PREPARATION TIME : 30 Minutes
COOKING TIME : 1 Hour 20 Minutes

*This recipe is a modernized version of a
basic country soup, containing meat, vegetables
and bread, which once served as a complete
meal. The ingredients are inexpensive and
simple to find year-round.*

INGREDIENTS

- ☐ 8oz smoked bacon
- ☐ ½ cabbage
- ☐ 2lbs turnips
- ☐ 1 onion
- ☐ 3 tbsps olive oil
- ☐ Bouquet garni (parsley, thyme, bay leaf)
- ☐ 10 black olives
- ☐ 1 French stick
- ☐ 1 cup double cream
- ☐ 6 sprigs chervil, chopped
- ☐ Salt and pepper

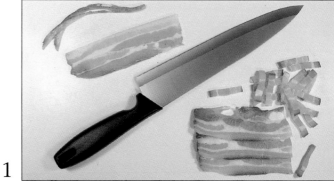

1 Cut off and reserve the rind of the bacon. Slice the meat into thin strips, then dice.

2 Place the bacon in a saucepan of cold water to cover, and bring to a boil. Rinse and drain in a sieve. Set aside.

3 Remove the outer leaves of the cabbage and slice thinly.

4 Blanch the cabbage strips for 4 minutes in boiling salted water. Rinse and drain in a sieve.

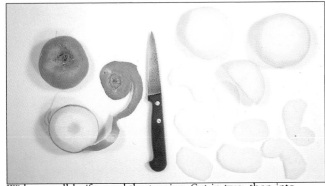

5 With a small knife, peel the turnips. Cut in two, then into smaller pieces.

6 Peel the onion, cut in two then chop finely.

7 Fry the onion in 2 tbsps hot oil. Add the bacon rind and the turnips. Cook, shaking often, for 5 minutes.

8 Add approximately 1½ litres/3 pints water or stock, the bouquet garni, salt and pepper. Cook, covered, over a moderate heat for 45 minutes.

9 Stone the olives and chop finely.

10 Remove the bacon from the soup and discard. Blend the soup smooth. Add the cabbage, and cook, stirring often, for 15 minutes over a low heat.

11 Slice the bread, and toast lightly. Brush with the remaining olive oil. Place in the oven for 1 minute.

12 Stir in the cream, smoked bacon pieces and chopped olives. Heat through and serve with the toasts. Sprinkle the soup with the chopped fresh chervil.

COLD MUSSEL SOUP

WITH

SAFFRON

SERVES : 6

PREPARATION TIME : 45 Minutes
COOKING TIME : 10 Minutes
CHILLING : 2 Hours

This is an elegant seafood soup perfect for warm summer evenings. Mussels and saffron are complementary flavors, and the use of real saffron threads is important. Crisp garlic croutons garnished with lumpfish roe complete the dish.

INGREDIENTS

- ☐ 4 cups mussels
- ☐ 2 shallots, finely chopped
- ☐ 1 cup white wine
- ☐ ½ cucumber
- ☐ 2 cups fish stock
- ☐ 1 cup heavy cream
- ☐ 1 pinch saffron powder
- ☐ 6 slices French bread
- ☐ 1 clove garlic
- ☐ 1 jar lumpfish roe
- ☐ 1½ tbsps chopped chives
- ☐ Saffron fronds
- ☐ Salt and pepper

1 Scrape and remove the beard from the mussels. Soak and wash them well. Ensure that the mussels are clean before going on to the next step.

2 Place the mussels in a large frying pan, add the shallots, pepper and white wine. Cook covered for 7 minutes.

3 Once the mussels are open and cool, remove from the shells.

4 Strain the cooking juices through a sieve lined with a piece of cheesecloth. Discard the sand and impurities.

5 Peel the cucumber lengthwise with a vegetable peeler.

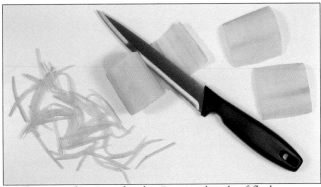

6 Cut the cucumber into chunks. Remove bands of flesh, working down to the centre and seeds. Cut the flesh into a fine julienne.

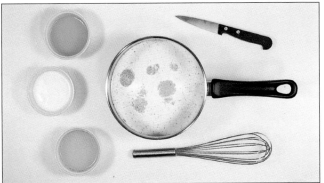

7 In a casserole, bring the stock, cooking juices, cream and saffron to a boil.

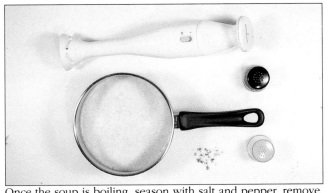

8 Once the soup is boiling, season with salt and pepper, remove it from the heat and blend until smooth. Allow to cool slightly, then refrigerate for 2 hours.

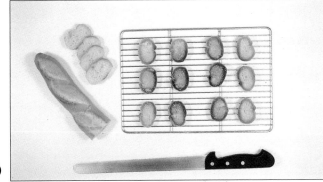

9 Toast the slices of bread evenly on each side.

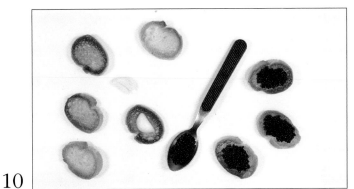

10 Remove the central shoot of the garlic. Rub the garlic over the toasts, and spoon some lumpfish roe over each slice.

11 Chop the chives.

12 Arrange all the ingredients together decoratively to present the soup. Sprinkle the saffron fronds over the soup just before serving.

CRAB SALAD

IN

ORANGE SHELLS

SERVES : 6

PREPARATION TIME : 35 Minutes

*This crab salad is attractively served in
hollowed-out orange shells for an original
presentation. The addition of the orange flesh
gives a contrasting sweet and sour taste to the
seafood and vegetables. Imitation crab meat
can be used, if desired.*

INGREDIENTS

- ☐ 3 large oranges (or 6 small)
- ☐ 1 avocado pear
- ☐ Juice of 1 lemon
- ☐ 1 egg yolk
- ☐ 1 tsp mustard
- ☐ 1 cup oil
- ☐ 1 tbsp tomato ketchup
- ☐ 1 tsp Cognac
- ☐ Few drops Tabasco
- ☐ 1 tsp Worcestershire sauce
- ☐ ½ onion
- ☐ 4oz small shrimp
- ☐ 10 (12oz) crab sticks
- ☐ 2 tomatoes
- ☐ ½ bunch chervil
- ☐ Salt and pepper

1 Halve the oranges and remove the flesh without crushing it. Reserve the shells for presentation.

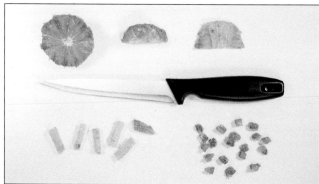

2 Cube the orange flesh.

3 Halve the avocado. Remove the stone, and peel. Dice, and coat with lemon juice to prevent discoloration.

4 Mix together the mustard, egg yolk, salt and pepper. Gradually whisk in the oil to make a mayonnaise.

5 When thick, add the ketchup, Cognac, Tabasco and Worcestershire sauce. Blend thoroughly.

6 Peel and halve the onion. Chop one half finely.

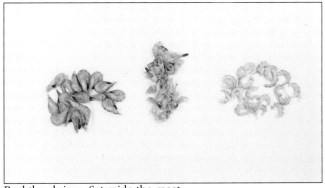

7 Peel the shrimp. Set aside the meat.

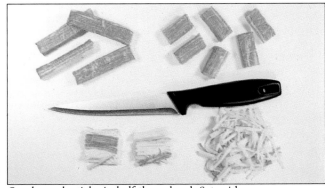

8 Cut the crab sticks in half then shred. Set aside.

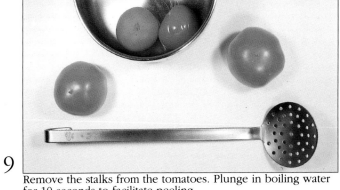

9 Remove the stalks from the tomatoes. Plunge in boiling water for 10 seconds to facilitate peeling.

10 Then plunge the tomatoes in cold water, peel off the skin, and cube the flesh. Discard the juice and seeds. Reserve 2 tbsps for decoration.

11 Mix all the ingredients into the mayonnaise, and check for seasoning.

12 Fill each orange shell with the salad, and garnish with the reserved tomato and chervil.

SPINACH SALAD

WITH

CHICKEN LIVERS

AND SWEETBREADS

SERVES : 6

PREPARATION TIME : 30 Minutes
COOKING TIME : 15 Minutes

A wonderfully healthy salad, rich in iron, that is easy to prepare and elegant to serve. The original sauce is a mayonnaise base thinned with stock and flavored with aromatic herbs.

INGREDIENTS

- ☐ 1 curly endive
- ☐ 2 small heads radicchio
- ☐ 5 cups fresh spinach
- ☐ 12oz lamb sweetbreads
- ☐ 1 sprig thyme
- ☐ 1 bay leaf
- ☐ 8oz chicken livers
- ☐ 1 egg yolk
- ☐ 1 tbsp mustard
- ☐ 1½ cups oil
- ☐ 3 tbsps fresh, chopped herbs
  (chives, tarragon, chervil)
- ☐ 1 carrot
- ☐ 1 tomato
- ☐ ¼ cup chicken stock
- ☐ 1 tbsp vinegar
- ☐ 2 tbsps butter
- ☐ Salt and pepper

1 Wash and trim the curly endive, spinach and radicchio. Slice the spinach into wide strips.

2 Blanch the sweetbreads in a flameproof casserole of salted water with the thyme and bay leaf. Bring to a boil and cook for 6 minutes. Remove and rinse.

3 Pull or cut the skin off the sweetbreads. Cut them into small pieces. Gently remove the veins from the chicken livers.

4 Make a mayonnaise by mixing together the egg yolk, mustard, salt and pepper. Gradually whisk in 1 cup of the oil.

5 When the mayonnaise has thickened, stir in 2 tbsps of chopped herbs (chives, tarragon, chervil). Mix well and set aside.

9 In a large frying pan, heat the remaining oil and the butter; when bubbling, sear the livers, then the sweetbreads.

6 Peel and slice the carrots thinly. Julienne the slices.

10 Shaking the pan continuously, continue to cook the livers and sweetbreads for 5 to 10 minutes. Season with salt and pepper and 1 tbsp of herbs. Set aside.

7 Carve around the heart of the tomato to remove only the flesh. Cut the flesh into strips, then cube.

11 Toss the spinach, curly endive and radicchio in a little of the mayonnaise. Serve the remaining mayonnaise in a small bowl.

8 Add the stock to the mayonnaise drop by drop, mixing in well, then stir in 1 tbsp of vinegar and the tomato cubes.

12 Spread a bed of salad on each plate, sprinkle over the carrot, and top with the livers and sweetbreads. Sprinkle with the remaining chopped herbs.

JELLIED CHICKEN TERRINE WITH VEGETABLE VINAIGRETTE

SERVES : 6

PREPARATION TIME : 35 Minutes
COOKING TIME : 1 Hour 15 Minutes
COOLING and CHILLING TIME : 10 Hours

A good entrée for entertaining, this is pretty to serve and can be prepared in advance. The terrine, based on chicken stock, contains diced vegetables and boned chicken. It's perfect for those counting their calories.

INGREDIENTS

- ☐ 3 carrots
- ☐ 2 zucchini
- ☐ 1 cup green beans, trimmed
- ☐ 1 cup peas, shelled
- ☐ 4 tbsps olive oil
- ☐ ½ onion, finely chopped
- ☐ 4 chicken legs
- ☐ 4 chicken livers
- ☐ Thyme
- ☐ Bay leaf
- ☐ 1 egg white, lightly beaten (5 seconds)
- ☐ 1½ sachets gelatine
- ☐ 1 tbsp wine vinegar
- ☐ 1 tsp coriander seeds, crushed
- ☐ Small bunch chives, chopped
- ☐ Small bunch chervil, chopped
- ☐ Salt and pepper

1 Cut the vegetables into sticks. Boil the vegetables individually in salted water : carrots (6 minutes), zucchini (3 minutes), green beans (8 minutes), peas (10 minutes). Refresh and drain.

2 In 1 tbsp oil sauté the onion, carrot trimmings, chicken meat, chicken livers, thyme, and bay leaf ; cover with water and cook for 35 minutes. Strain the stock through a sieve.

3 Pour the warm stock onto the egg white and mix well. Stir and bring to a boil in a saucepan. Cook for 10 minutes, then strain through a cheesecloth-lined sieve.

4 Soften the gelatine in a little water, and stir into 2 cups hot stock. Season and allow to cool for 30 minutes.

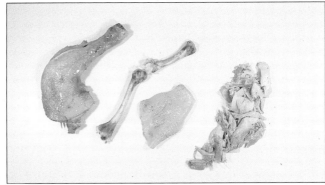

5 Take the chicken meat off the bone and chop finely. Chop the skin finely.

9 Make a vinaigrette by mixing together the vinegar, salt, pepper, crushed coriander, chives and 3 tbsps olive oil. Set aside.

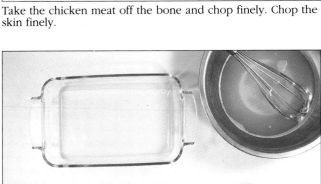

6 Fill the base of your mold or terrine with a layer of the stock, and leave in the refrigerator until firm.

10 Mix the reserved vegetables into the vinaigrette. Adjust seasoning. Set aside.

7 Distribute a layer of cut vegetables over the jellied stock. Add a layer of stock, then a layer of meat. Allow to set in the refrigerator.

11 When the terrine has set (8 to 10 hours), dip the base of the mold in hot water for 30 seconds and unmold. Cut into thin slices.

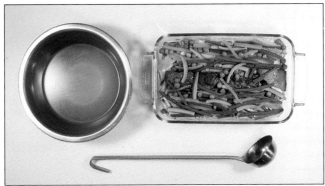

8 Reserve 3 tbsps of the vegetables and dice. Layer the remaining vegetables, the chicken livers and another layer of stock into the terrine. Chill until firm.

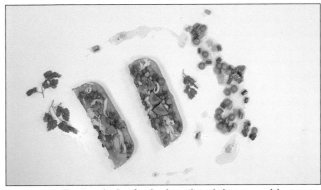

12 Serve garnished with the fresh chervil and the vegetable vinaigrette.

SHRIMP SALAD

WITH

BACON

SERVES : 6

PREPARATION TIME : 40 Minutes
COOKING TIME : 25 Minutes

*An attractive first course or a good luncheon
dish if the quantities are increased. The
vinaigrette sauce is quite unique, flavored with
a reduction of shrimp shells cooked in olive oil.*

INGREDIENTS

- ☐ 36 medium shrimp
- ☐ 1 carrot
- ☐ ½ onion
- ☐ ¼ leek
- ☐ 3 tbsps olive oil
- ☐ 4oz lamb's lettuce
- ☐ 1 head fancy lettuce
- ☐ 4 slices bread
- ☐ 1 clove garlic (central shoot removed)
- ☐ 6oz bacon, finely sliced
- ☐ ½ cucumber
- ☐ 1 tbsp wine vinegar
- ☐ ½ bunch chives
- ☐ 1½ tbsps butter
- ☐ Salt and pepper
- ☐ Fresh herbs (chives)

1 Peel the shrimp, and remove the heads and tails (reserve). Devein.

2 Peel and roughly chop the carrot, leek and onion.

3 Fry the vegetables with the shrimp trimmings and half the peelings in 1 tbsp of oil. Pour in 1 cup water, and cook over a moderate heat for 10 to 15 minutes.

4 Trim, and wash the lamb's lettuce and the inner leaves of the fancy lettuce.

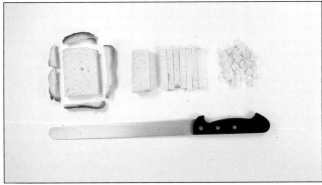

5 Trim the crusts off the bread. Cut into cubes.

6 Halve the garlic, and gently heat in 1 tbsp of oil. Add the bread cubes, and sauté to make croutons. When the bread cubes are golden brown, drain on kitchen paper.

7 Stack the bacon slices and cut them into small, neat strips.

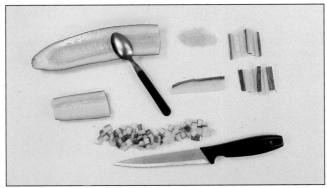

8 Halve the cucumber lengthwise. Peel and remove the seeds with a small spoon. Slice the flesh and then dice.

9 Strain the shrimp stock through a fine sieve lined with cheesecloth. Measure out ½ cup.

10 When the stock is cool, whisk in 1 tbsp oil, the vinegar, salt and pepper to taste, and the chopped chives. Set aside.

11 Sauté the shrimp and bacon in the butter for 2 minutes. Add a little pepper. Set aside.

12 Serve the mixed salad topped with the shrimp, bacon and croutons. Sprinkle over the cucumber and dress with the vinaigrette. Garnish with fresh, chopped herbs.

ROQUEFORT TIMBALES

WITH

FRESH FIGS

SERVES : 6

PREPARATION TIME : 30 Minutes
COOKING TIME : 40 Minutes

Here is a most original flavor combination which is absolutely delicious. These cheese-flavored egg and cream timbales can be served to begin the meal, or as a cheese and fruit course after the main dish.

INGREDIENTS

- ☐ ¾ cup Roquefort cheese (or other blue cheese)
- ☐ 2 cups milk
- ☐ Nutmeg
- ☐ 4 eggs
- ☐ 2 tsps butter
- ☐ 10 fresh figs
- ☐ 6 servings fancy lettuce
- ☐ ½ bunch chives
- ☐ 20 hazelnuts
- ☐ 1 tomato
- ☐ 1 shallot
- ☐ 1 tbsp vinegar
- ☐ 3 tbsps oil
- ☐ Salt and pepper

1 Roughly chop the cheese or crumble with a fork.

2 Bring the milk to a boil with a little salt, pepper and grated nutmeg.

3 Beat the eggs. Whisk the hot milk into the eggs.

4 Add the cheese to the milk and eggs and stir well.

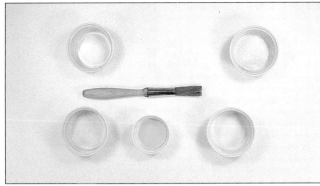

5 Grease 6 ramekins with the butter, then fill almost to the top with the milk and egg mixture.

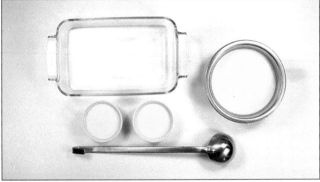

6 Bake the timbales in a tray of water in a moderate oven, 350°F for 35 minutes.

7 Cut the stems off the figs. Slice and then cube the flesh.

8 Wash and trim the lettuce. Dry it well. Chop the chives.

9 Shell the hazelnuts and scrape off the inner skin. Chop the nuts finely.

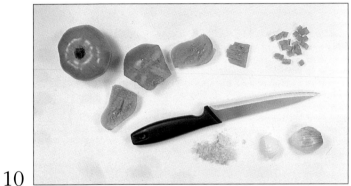

10 Peel the tomato, and chop only the outer flesh. Finely chop the shallot.

11 Make a vinaigrette by whisking together the salt, vinegar, pepper, chives, shallot, hazelnuts and oil.

12 When the timbales are cooked, run a knife around the inside edges of the ramekins, and turn out. Serve on a bed of lettuce, dotted with the figs, and dressed with the vinaigrette.

CREPES FILLED

WITH

VEGETABLES

SERVES : 6

PREPARATION TIME : 1 Hour
COOKING TIME : 50 Minutes
RESTING TIME : 35 Minutes

A completely vegetarian dish which can be served as a first course or, in larger quantities, as a main dish. Delicate buckwheat crepes are filled with steamed diced vegetables. The rich chive-butter sauce can be served sparingly on the side for those watching their diet.

INGREDIENTS

- ☐ 2½ cups buckwheat flour
- ☐ 2 eggs
- ☐ 3 cups milk
- ☐ 3 tbsps butter, melted
- ☐ 2 carrots
- ☐ 2 medium zucchini
- ☐ 1lb 2oz fresh lima beans
- ☐ 1 cup fresh peas
- ☐ ½ cup bean sprouts
- ☐ ½ cup canned corn
- ☐ 2 tbsps oil
- ☐ ½ egg, beaten
- ☐ 3 shallots, chopped
- ☐ ½ cup white wine
- ☐ ¾ cup butter
- ☐ Small bunch chives, chopped
- ☐ ½ lemon
- ☐ Fresh herbs (chervil)
- ☐ Salt and pepper

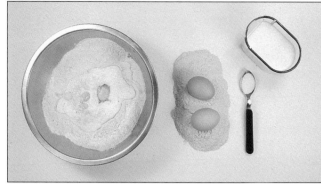

1 Prepare the pancake batter by beating together the buckwheat flour, 1 tsp salt and the eggs. Gradually mix in the milk.

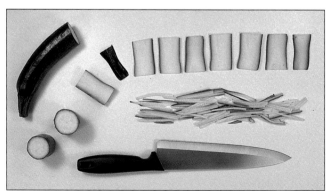

2 Add half the melted butter. Mix in well. Set aside to rest for approximately 35 minutes.

3 Peel and slice the carrots finely. Cut the slices into thin matchsticks.

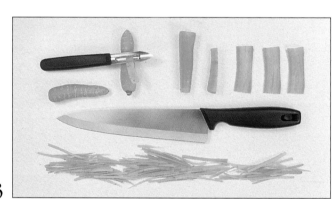

4 Trim the ends of the zucchini. Cut into chunks, slices and then into matchsticks.

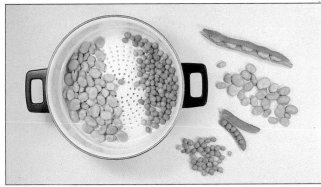

5 Shell the peas and the lima beans. Steam together for 10 minutes, beginning with the peas, and 3 minutes later adding the beans. After cooking, remove the skins of the lima beans.

6 Steam the carrots for 4 minutes, and the zucchini for 3 minutes.

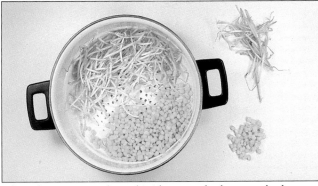

7 When the carrots and zucchini have cooked, steam the bean sprouts and the corn for 5 minutes. Remove and set aside.

8 Mix all the cooked vegetables together, and season with salt and pepper. Add the remaining melted butter, and mix in well so all the vegetables are coated. Set aside.

9 Fry the crepes lightly on each side in an oiled frying pan. Use paper towels to oil the pan lightly before pouring in the batter for each crepe.

10 Fill each crepe with some of the vegetable mixture. Fold up, and seal the folds with beaten egg.

11 In a saucepan reduce the white wine, shallots for 15 minutes. Whisk in the butter gradually. Add the chopped chives and a squeeze of lemon juice. Keep warm over hot water.

12 Reheat the crepes on a lightly buttered, non-stick baking tray in a warm oven for 10 minutes. Serve the filled crepes garnished with the chive-butter sauce. Garnish with chervil.

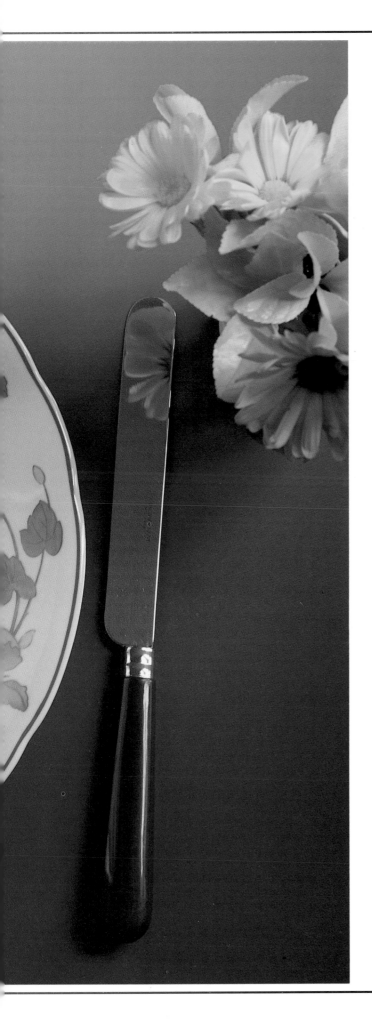

MIXED SEAFOOD TART

SERVES : 6

PREPARATION TIME : 45 Minutes
COOKING TIME : 35 Minutes

This is a seafood variation of the basic quiche. A pie shell is filled with a cheese custard and a mixture of mussels, shrimp and clams. Serve small slices as a first course or larger ones for a main dish, accompanied with a tossed green salad.

INGREDIENTS

- ☐ 2½ cups flour
- ☐ ¼ cup water
- ☐ 1 egg yolk
- ☐ ½ cup butter at room temperature
- ☐ 4 cups mussels
- ☐ 1lb cockles
- ☐ 1 cup white wine
- ☐ 8oz medium cooked shrimp
- ☐ 12oz small scallops
- ☐ 1 cup milk
- ☐ 1½ cups cream
- ☐ 4 eggs
- ☐ 1 cup grated Gruyère cheese
- ☐ Nutmeg
- ☐ Butter
- ☐ Fresh herbs (dill)
- ☐ Salt and pepper

1 Make the dough by mixing together the flour, the water, salt and egg yolk

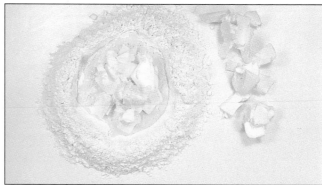

2 Add the softened butter, and mix into the dough completely.

3 Work the dough into a ball, and allow to rest in the refrigerator for 30 minutes.

4 Rinse and rub clean the mussels and cockles. Use several changes of water to eliminate all the sand.

5 Place the mussels and cockles in separate saucepans, each containing half of the wine. Cover and cook until the shells open, approximately 5 minutes. Allow to cool.

6 Shell the shrimp. Cut into small pieces. Wash the scallops, and discard the coral. Remove the mussels and cockles from their shells.

7 In a bowl, mix together the milk, cream, eggs, grated cheese, salt, pepper, and a few gratings of nutmeg. Set aside.

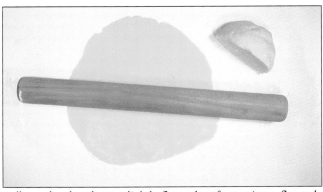

8 Roll out the dough on a lightly floured surface using a floured rolling pin.

9 Use the dough to line a greased pie pan. Trim off the excess dough. Prick the base of the dough with a fork.

10 Drain all excess liquid from the seafood. Arrange with the uncooked sea scallops in the bottom of the pie shell.

11 Pour over the custard mixture, and cook in a very hot oven 475°F for 25 minutes. Cover with a sheet of foil, if necessary.

12 Remove from the pie pan, and serve warm, cut into wedges. Accompany with a tossed, mixed lettuce salad, if desired. Garnish with dill.

STUFFED EGGS À LA PROVENÇALE

SERVES : 6

PREPARATION TIME : 40 Minutes
COOKING TIME : 30 Minutes

Hard-boiled eggs are halved and refilled with the yolks mixed with anchovies. Provençale ingredients traditionally include garlic and tomatoes. In this case it refers to the vegetable side dish of onion, peppers and tomatoes.

INGREDIENTS

- ☐ 9 eggs
- ☐ 6 anchovy fillets (in oil)
- ☐ 4 peppers (2 red, 2 green)
- ☐ 2 onions
- ☐ 2 cloves garlic (central shoot removed)
- ☐ 1 chili pepper
- ☐ 1 egg yolk
- ☐ 1 tsp mustard
- ☐ 1 cup olive oil
- ☐ 8 green olives
- ☐ 1 tbsp wine vinegar
- ☐ Fresh herbs (chervil)
- ☐ Salt and pepper

1 Hard-boil the eggs for 10 minutes. Cool in cold water.

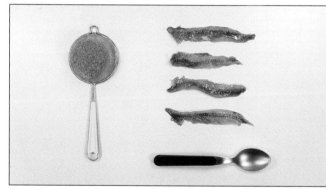

2 Shell the eggs, cut in half lengthwise and remove the yolks, with a stainless steel knife. Press the yolks through a fine sieve. Set aside the whites.

3 Bone the anchovy fillets if necessary and push them through a fine sieve. Set aside.

4 Cut open the peppers, and remove all seeds and pith. Cut into even-sized slices.

5

Peel and chop the onions with the garlic. Slice open the chili pepper and remove the seeds.

6

Fry the onion, half of the garlic, the chili pepper and peppers in 3½ tbsp olive oil for 15 minutes, stirring frequently. Season with salt and pepper, and set aside to cool.

7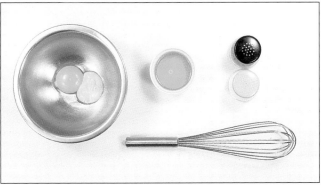

Make the mayonnaise. Mix together one raw egg yolk, the mustard, salt and pepper. Whisk in the remaining oil gradually.

8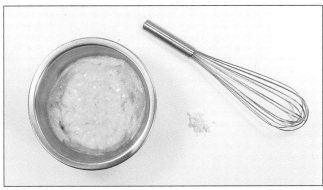

Add the remaining chopped garlic to the mayonnaise. Mix in well and chill.

9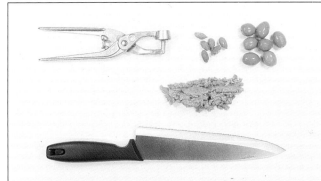

Stone the olives, and chop finely.

10

Stir the cooked egg yolks, the anchovy paste, and the chopped olives into the mayonnaise. Beat in the vinegar.

11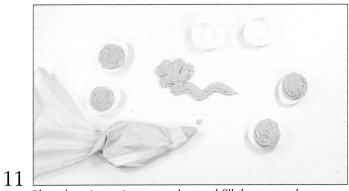

Place the mixture in a pastry bag and fill the reserved egg whites decoratively.

12

Serve the stuffed eggs on top of the cooled pepper and onion mixture (remove the chili pepper). Garnish with the fresh chervil.

LASAGNE

WITH

SEAFOOD

SERVES : 6

PREPARATION TIME : 1 Hour 30 Minutes
COOKING TIME : 1 Hour 15 Minutes

*Home-made lasagne pasta is layered with
mussels, cockles and shrimp in an aromatic
tomato sauce and topped with shredded Swiss
cheese. This dish can be prepared in advance
and reheated. If time is short, use commercially
prepared lasagne noodles.*

INGREDIENTS

- ☐ 1lb flour
- ☐ 4 eggs
- ☐ 4 tbsps olive oil
- ☐ 1lb cockles
- ☐ 4 cups mussels
- ☐ 1lb shrimp
- ☐ 1 cup white wine
- ☐ 2 shallots, chopped
- ☐ 1 onion, finely chopped
- ☐ 2 cloves garlic, chopped
- ☐ 6 tomatoes, skinned, seeded and crushed
- ☐ 2 tbsps chopped parsley
- ☐ 3 tbsps butter, melted
- ☐ ½ cup Gruyère cheese, shredded
- ☐ Fresh herbs (chervil)
- ☐ Salt and pepper

1 In a bowl, mix together the flour, 1 tsp salt and the eggs with your fingers to form into a dough. Shape into a ball.

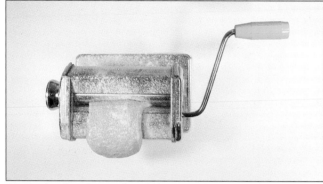

2 Divide the dough into 4 and flatten each piece before passing it through the rollers of a pasta machine.

3 Continue rolling until long, thin strips of pasta are formed. Flour frequently during the process. Cut into small rectangles and leave to dry for 2 hours.

4 Cook the lasagne sheets a few at a time in boiling, salted water with 1 tbsp of oil, for 3 minutes each.

5 Remove and refresh under cold water, then lay on a damp kitchen towel until needed.

6 Wash and scrub the cockles and mussels. Change the water frequently as you wash. Peel the shrimp and cut into pieces.

7 Pour the wine into a casserole, add the shallots, cockles, and cook, covered, on a high heat until they open. Remove. Cook the mussels in the same liquid until they open. Shell both.

8 Fry the onions and garlic in 3 tbsps olive oil in a frying pan. Add the tomato and 1 tbsp parsley. Strain the stock from the shellfish through a sieve lined with cheesecloth.

9 Add the shrimp cockles and mussels, with their cooking liquid, to the pan. Cook over a moderate heat for 20 minutes.

10 Brush an ovenproof baking pan with some of the butter. Layer the sheets of lasagne with the seafood mixture. Brush the pasta with butter each time.

11 Finish with a layer of lasagne, brush with butter. Sprinkle over the cheese and remaining parsley. Cover with foil and bake in a hot oven 450°F for 25 minutes.

12 Remove the foil. Brown the top of the lasagne under a broiler for 5 minutes. Serve cut into portions, garnished with the chopped chervil.

SPAGHETTI

WITH

CRAB AND BACON

SERVES : 6

PREPARATION TIME : 1 Hour
COOKING TIME : 20 Minutes

This recipe includes a wonderful preparation of home-made parsley pasta. It is tossed and served with a seafood sauce, fresh or imitation crab and bacon.

INGREDIENTS

- ☐ 1 bunch parsley (approximately 6 tbsps)
- ☐ 1lb 2oz flour
- ☐ 4 eggs
- ☐ 8oz bacon, in one piece
- ☐ 1 tbsp olive oil
- ☐ 10 (12oz) crab sticks
- ☐ 1½ cups heavy cream
- ☐ 3 tbsps butter
- ☐ Fresh herbs (chervil)
- ☐ Salt and pepper

1 Trim the leaves off the parsley. Cook for 10 minutes in boiling water. Pass through a fine sieve and reserve the cooking liquid.

2 Purée the parsley with 3 tbsps of the cooking liquid in a blender.

3 In a bowl, mix together the flour, salt, eggs and 1½ tbsps parsley purée. Form into a ball.

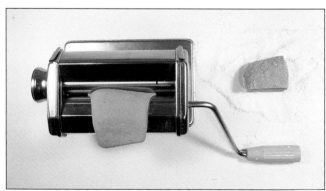

4 Quarter the dough and form these pieces into balls. Press each ball flat and run it through a pasta machine.

5 Thin the dough progressively by passing it through the machine several times. Flour the dough frequently throughout the operation.

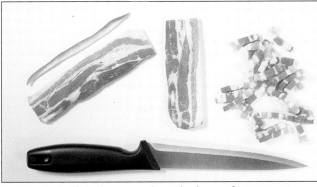

6 Run the flattened strips of dough through the spaghetti cutter.

7 Cut the rind off the bacon and cut the bacon first into strips, and then into small rectangles.

8 Add the olive oil to boiling, salted water and cook the spaghetti for 5 minutes. Strain and rinse.

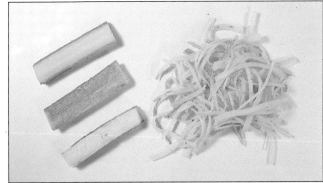

9 Shred the crab sticks with your fingers.

10 Heat the cream gently with the crab and bacon pieces.

11 Meanwhile, heat the butter in a pan and when it bubbles, add the spaghetti (first reheated by plunging for 30 seconds in boiling water). Mix well and season with salt and pepper.

12 Place the buttered spaghetti around the edges of the dinner plates and arrange the crab/bacon mixture in the center. Garnish with chopped fresh herbs.

CHINESE NOODLES

WITH

VEGETABLES

SERVES : 6

PREPARATION TIME : 50 Minutes
COOKING TIME : 20 Minutes

This is an Oriental-inspired vegetarian preparation of Chinese noodles. They are mixed with bamboo shoots, black mushrooms and cucumber and a light sauce consisting of a reduction of the cooking juices.

INGREDIENTS

- ☐ 2 tbsp dried black Chinese mushrooms
- ☐ 3 slices fresh ginger root
- ☐ 1 clove garlic (central shoot removed)
- ☐ 2 carrots
- ☐ ¼ cucumber
- ☐ 1 jar bamboo shoots (approximately 1 cup)
- ☐ ½ cup bean sprouts
- ☐ 14oz Chinese noodles
- ☐ 3 tbsps olive oil
- ☐ 1 small chili pepper
- ☐ 5 tbsps soy sauce
- ☐ 1 tbsp honey
- ☐ Fresh herbs (chives)
- ☐ Salt and pepper

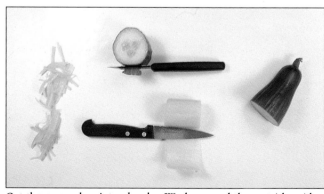

1 Soak the mushrooms for 15 minutes to reconstitute them. Trim off the sandy stump, and boil the mushrooms for 5 minutes.

2 Peel the ginger root with a vegetable peeler, cut off 3 slices, and chop finely. Chop the garlic finely.

3 Peel the carrots and cut into matchsticks. Squeeze out the water from the mushrooms, and slice into matchsticks.

4 Cut the cucumber into chunks. Work around the outside with a knife to obtain thick slices of peel, then cut the slices into matchsticks.

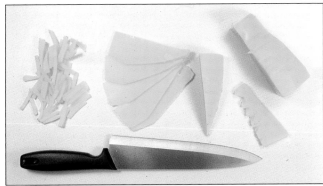

5 Trim the bamboo shoots. Cut into slices then into matchsticks.

6 Rinse, then blanch the bamboo shoots for 2 minutes. Set aside to drain thoroughly.

7 Trim, and wash the bean sprouts. Blanch for 1 minute. Plunge into cold water, and set aside to drain thoroughly.

8 Cook the noodles in boiling salted water for a few minutes, depending on the thickness of the noodles. Drain, rinse, and set aside to drain thoroughly.

9 In a frying pan, heat the oil, and fry the ginger, garlic and chili pepper for several seconds.

10 Add the bamboo shoots, mushrooms and carrots. Fry for 4 minutes, then add the bean sprouts. Cook for another 2 minutes.

11 Add the noodles, soy sauce and honey. Stir well, and heat through.

12 At the last moment, add the cucumber. Heat for 1 minute. Remove the chili pepper, garnish with the herbs, and serve.

TAGLIATELLE

WITH

BLUE CHEESE

SERVES : 6

PREPARATION TIME : 1 Hour
COOKING TIME : 15 Minutes
DRYING : 2 Hours

Freshly made pasta noodles are tossed with a creamy sauce flavored with blue cheese and diced dried apricots. The fruit and cheese mixture marries well to give a sweet and savoury dish. It is garnished with pine nuts to add texture and taste.

INGREDIENTS

- [ ] 1lb 2oz flour
- [ ] 5 eggs
- [ ] 1 tbsp olive oil
- [ ] 4oz blue cheese
  (Roquefort, Stilton)
- [ ] 1 cup dried apricots
  (or other dried fruit)
- [ ] 1¼ cups heavy cream
- [ ] ¼ cup milk
- [ ] 2 egg yolks
- [ ] ¼ cup pine nuts
- [ ] ½ bunch chives
- [ ] Salt and pepper

1 In a bowl, work together the flour, salt and eggs, to form a soft ball of dough.

2 Quarter the dough and flatten each piece. Dredge each piece with plenty of flour. Flour the rollers of a pasta machine, and either pass the dough through the machine or roll it out.

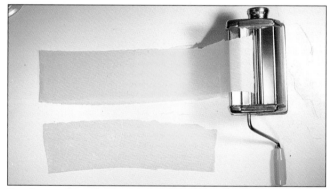

3 Continue rolling the pasta until thin. Flour frequently during the process.

4 Thread the dough strips through the tagliatelle cutter, or cut into strips with a knife. Dredge the noodles with flour and allow to dry for 2 hours.

5 Bring to a boil a saucepan of salted water with 1 tbsp oil. Cook the pasta for 2 to 4 minutes, stirring with a fork.

6 Drain the tagliatelle and rinse in plenty of cold water to prevent sticking. Set aside.

7 Break up the cheese and force through a sieve with the back of a spoon.

8 Cut the apricots into strips then dice.

9 Slowly heat the cream in a saucepan. Stir in the cheese and milk. Blend until smooth with a hand-held electric blender.

10 Whilst the sauce is hot, stir in the tagliatelle, and apricots, and season again, as necessary. Heat through quickly, so the cream does not curdle nor the noodles overcook.

11 Mix the pasta with two forks. Remove from the heat, and mix in the egg yolks and the pine nuts.

12 Chop the chives finely and sprinkle them over the tagliatelle ; serve immediately.

RABBIT RAVIOLI

WITH

TARRAGON

SERVES : 6

PREPARATION TIME : 1 Hour 30 Minutes
COOKING TIME : 1 Hour 50 Minutes

*A time-consuming pasta dish well worth the
effort. Home-made ravioli are filled with a
mixture of ground rabbit meat and fresh
tarragon. The light sauce is a reduction of the
cooking liquid enhanced with cream and
tarragon.*

INGREDIENTS

☐ 3 cups flour
☐ 3 eggs
☐ ½ leek
☐ 1 onion, finely chopped
☐ 1 carrot
☐ 2 tbsps olive oil
☐ 3 rabbit thighs
☐ 5 sprigs tarragon
☐ 1 bouquet garni (parsley, thyme, bay leaf)
☐ 1 egg, beaten
☐ ¼ cup heavy cream
☐ Salt and pepper

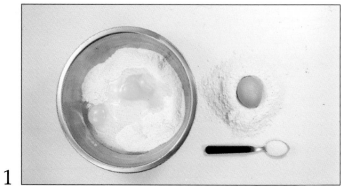

1 Place the flour in a bowl with 1 tsp salt. Add the eggs. Mix with your fingers to make a dough and form into a ball. Set aside to rest.

2 Wash and dice the leek, onion and carrot. Set aside.

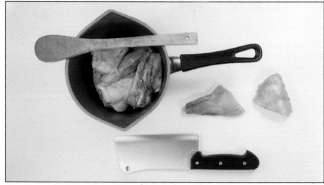

3 Fry the rabbit in the oil until lightly colored.

4 Remove the tarragon leaves from three sprigs, reserve the stalks for the stock, and chop the leaves.

5 Add the onion, carrot, leek, tarragon stalks and bouquet garni to the rabbit. Cook for 2 minutes. Add 3 cups water. Cook covered on a low heat for 1 hour 30 minutes.

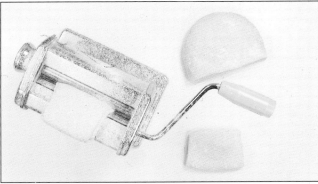

6 When cooked, remove the rabbit thighs, bone, and mince the meat. Mix with 3/4 of the tarragon leaves. Season with salt and pepper. Strain the stock through a fine sieve and set it aside.

7 Divide the dough into smaller, flat rounds, and thread these through a pasta machine to form thin pasta strips.

8 Cut the pasta into rectangles. Mix 2 tbsps stock into the meat and tarragon, and place about a teaspoon of the mixture in the center of each rectangle.

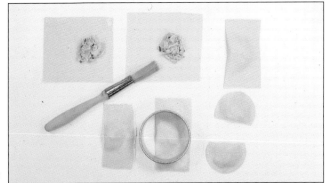

9 Brush the edges of the rectangles with beaten egg and fold over one side. Pinch the edges together with your fingers, then, using a pastry cutter, shape into rounds. Set aside.

10 Cook the ravioli for 5 minutes in salted, boiling water with 1 sprig tarragon. Drain with a slotted spoon, then place on a damp kitchen towel.

11 Reduce 1 1/2 cups rabbit stock by half, add the cream and remaining tarragon. Blend smooth, heat through and season.

12 Serve the ravioli and cream sauce in soup plates. Garnish with the remaining chopped tarragon.

PASTA

WITH

LEEKS

AND MUSSELS

SERVES : 6

PREPARATION TIME : 30 Minutes
COOKING TIME : 25 Minutes

This pasta dish is relatively quick and easy to prepare. Spiral-shaped pasta is tossed with cooked mussels and sautéed leeks in a sauce of the reduced cooking juices. The thinly sliced ham adds flavor and makes an attractive garnish.

INGREDIENTS

- ☐ 3 cups mussels
- ☐ ½ cup white wine
- ☐ 1 shallot, chopped
- ☐ 2 medium-sized leeks
- ☐ ¾ cup heavy cream
- ☐ 1lb spiral-shaped pasta
- ☐ 1 tbsp oil
- ☐ 2 slices ham
- ☐ 1½ tbsps butter
- ☐ Fresh herbs (chives)
- ☐ Salt and pepper

1 Scrub the mussels; remove the beards and wash in several changes of water to eliminate the sand.

2 In a large, covered saucepan, cook the mussels in the white wine with the chopped shallot for approximately 5 minutes, over a high heat.

3 Cool, and remove the opened mussels from their shells. Reserve the cooking liquid.

4 Quarter each leek lengthwise, wash thoroughly, and slice finely.

5 In a covered saucepan, cook the leeks in the cream with salt and pepper to taste for 10 minutes over a low heat.

6 In a large casserole of water, boil the pasta with 1 tbsp oil. Stir the pasta as it cooks, to prevent sticking.

7 Drain after 5 or 6 minutes. Rinse in cold water to prevent sticking.

8 Remove any fat or rind from the ham, and slice into small pieces.

9 Strain the mussel cooking liquid through a sieve lined with cheesecloth. Measure out approximately ½ cup.

10 Add the shelled mussels and the mussel liquid to the cream mixture, and cook for 4 minutes, stirring constantly.

11 Melt the butter in a deep frying pan, and reheat the pasta gently with the ham. Season to taste.

12 When the pasta is heated through, add the cream and leek sauce, and serve garnished with the chopped chives.

POTATO

AND

LAMB CASSEROLE AU GRATIN

SERVES : 6

PREPARATION TIME : 45 Minutes
COOKING TIME : 1 Hour 30 Minutes

A wonderful lunch or supper dish which can be prepared ahead and reheated. Sliced potatoes are layered with a filling of ground lamb and onion, topped with shredded Swiss cheese and browned in the oven. Serve hot or at room temperature with a green salad.

POTATO AND LAMB CASSEROLE AU GRATIN

INGREDIENTS

- ☐ 2¹/₂lbs potatoes
- ☐ 1¹/₄lbs lamb shoulder boned
- ☐ 1 egg
- ☐ 1 clove garlic (central shoot removed)
- ☐ 4 sprigs parsley
- ☐ 2 cups milk
- ☐ 2 tomatoes
- ☐ 2 onions
- ☐ 4 slices white bread
- ☐ 2 tbsps olive oil
- ☐ 2 cups chicken or vegetable stock
- ☐ ¹/₂ cup Gruyère cheese, shredded
- ☐ 4 servings mixed lettuce, washed and trimmed
- ☐ 4 tbsps vinaigrette sauce
- ☐ Fresh basil (optional)
- ☐ Salt and pepper

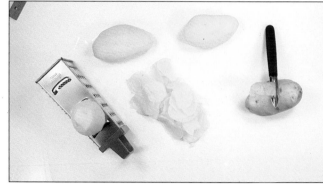

1 Peel the potatoes and slice them very thinly. Use a grater if available.

2 Cut the lamb in pieces. Place the meat in a food processor with the egg, and season with salt and pepper. Process finely.

3 Chop the garlic finely. Wash, trim and finely chop the parsley.

4 Add the garlic and parsley to the meat. Add the milk and mix well.

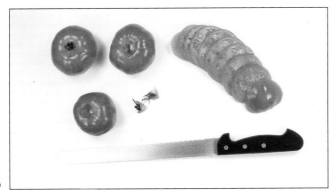

5 Cut the core out of the tomatoes and slice thinly with a serrated knife.

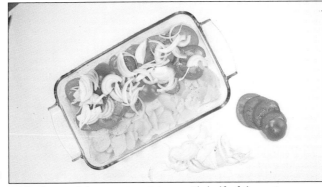

9 Add a layer of the tomato mixture with half of the onion.

6 Peel and cut the onions in half. Slice very thinly. Set aside.

10 Add the meat mixture, then the remaining onion. Pour in the stock.

7 Place the bread in a food processor, and process to obtain fine breadcrumbs.

11 Layer the remaining potato over the meat and onion. Top with the breadcrumbs and cheese. Cover with foil, cook in a hot oven 425⁰F for 1 hour 30 minutes.

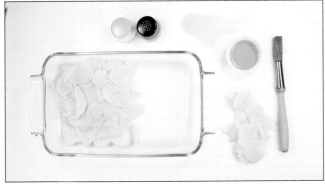

8 Oil the base of a gratin dish (or ovenproof pan), and distribute half of the potato over this. Season well.

12 Halfway through the baking period, remove the foil. Serve with a mixed green salad dressed with a classic vinaigrette. Decorate with fresh basil, if desired.

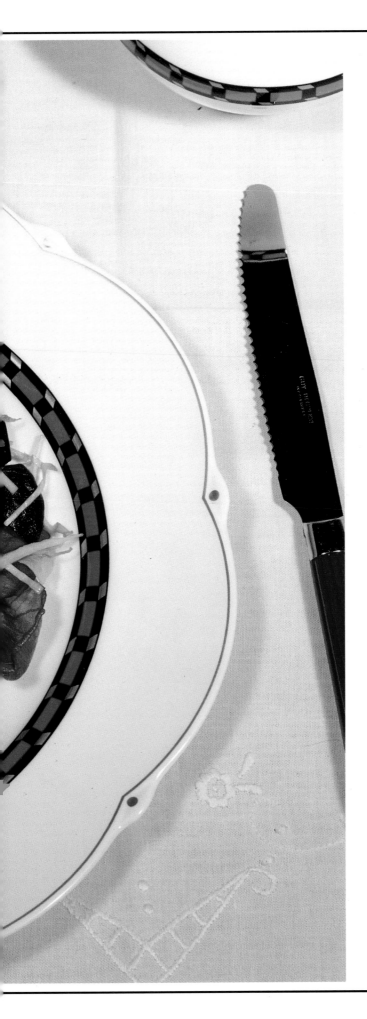

BAKED POTATO PANCAKE

WITH

RATATOUILLE

SERVES : 6

PREPARATION TIME : 50 Minutes
COOKING TIME : 25 Minutes

This dish is rather elaborate to prepare, but makes an original and delicious vegetarian appetizer or luncheon dish. Thinly sliced potatoes are filled with a flavorful vegetable preparation of onion, eggplant and tomato, and baked in the oven.

INGREDIENTS

- ☐ 1 onion
- ☐ 1 clove garlic (in method)
- ☐ 1 eggplant
- ☐ 2 zucchinis
- ☐ 2 peppers (1 red and 1 green)
- ☐ 2 tomatoes
- ☐ 4 tbsps olive oil
- ☐ Bouquet garni (parsley, thyme, bay leaf)
- ☐ 1 egg
- ☐ 2¼lbs medium potatoes
- ☐ Salt and pepper

1 Peel and slice the onion finely. Halve the garlic, remove the central shoot and chop finely.

2 Trim the zucchini and eggplant. Cut into slices, sticks and then cubes.

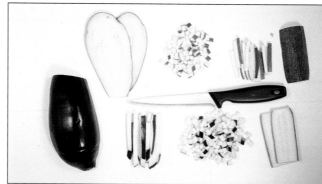

3 Cut open the peppers, remove all white pith and seeds, and dice.

4 Remove the stalks of the tomatoes. Plunge for 10 seconds in boiling water. Refresh immediately in cold water.

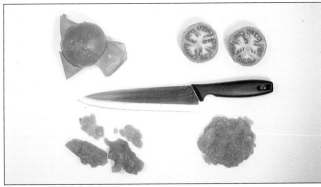

5 Peel off the skins, halve, seed and roughly chop.

6 In a frying pan, heat 2 tbsps of oil and fry the garlic ; add the diced vegetables (except the tomatoes) and cook for 5 minutes, stirring. Add the tomato and bouquet garni.

7 Season the ratatouille with salt and pepper. After 10 minutes, the liquid should have evaporated. Cool, then stir in the egg. Set aside.

8 Peel and rinse the potatoes. Trim into smooth cylinder shapes. Slice thinly with a knife or a grater.

9 Oil a frying pan, and arrange half of the potatoes in a neat rose shape. Season with salt and pepper.

10 Spread the ratatouille over the potatoes, covering well.

11 Cover the ratatouille with another layer of potatoes. Bake, uncovered, in a hot oven 400°F for 20 minutes.

12 Remove from the oven and turn out onto a serving plate. Serve as a first course with a tossed salad, or as a side dish with meat.

BASMATI RICE

WITH

VEGETABLES

SERVES : 6

PREPARATION TIME : 45 Minutes
COOKING TIME : 30 Minutes

*A vegetarian rice dish which can be served by
itself or as an accompaniment to meat and fish.
The rice is mixed with diced carrots, zucchini
and peppers, and is flavored with exotic Indian
spices. The basmati rice can be replaced with
ordinary rice, but the taste is not as good.*

INGREDIENTS

☐ 2 peppers (1 green, 1 red)
☐ 1 zucchini
☐ 1 carrot
☐ 2 shallots
☐ ½ vanilla bean
☐ 2 pinches cinnamon
☐ 1 pinch saffron
☐ ½ tsp turmeric
☐ ½ tsp curry powder
☐ 3 cardamom seeds
☐ 3 tbsps olive oil
☐ 1²/₃ cups basmati rice
☐ 1 bouquet garni (parsley, thyme, bay leaf)
☐ Fresh chervil
☐ Salt and pepper

1 Trim the stem from the peppers, cut them open and remove all white pith and seeds.

2 Cut peppers into even-sized strips.

3 Cut the zucchini into chunks, then slices, and finally matchsticks.

4 Cut the carrot into slightly smaller matchsticks.

5
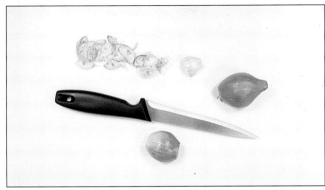
Peel the shallots, halve lengthwise, and chop finely.

6

Slit open the vanilla bean, run the back of the knife down the inside to extract the seeds. Tie the parsley, thyme and bay leaf into a bouquet garni.

7
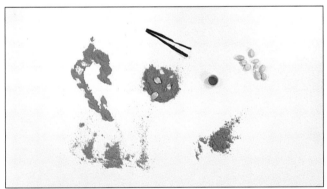
Mix together the cinnamon, saffron, turmeric, curry powder, cardamom, and vanilla bean.

8

In an ovenproof frying pan, heat the oil and sauté the vegetables for 5 minutes, stirring frequently, with a spatula.

9

When cooked through, add the rice and bouquet garni.

10

Fry the rice until transparent. Measure water 1½ times the volume of the rice and stir the spices into the water.

11

Add the water and spices to the rice (do not stir again). Cover and cook in a hot oven 425°F for 25 minutes.

12

Fluff the rice up with a fork and serve garnished with the chervil.

RICE PILAF

WITH

MIXED SEAFOOD

SERVES : 6

PREPARATION TIME : 45 Minutes
COOKING TIME : 40 Minutes

Rice is cooked pilaf style in a seafood stock. It is mixed with a variety of seafood and a creamy herb sauce. The different seafoods can be varied according to your taste and the availability of fresh ingredients.

INGREDIENTS

☐ 2 shallots
☐ 6oz mushrooms
☐ 1¼ cups white wine
☐ 6 large clams, well washed
☐ 4 cups mussels, well washed
☐ 5 sprigs of parsley
☐ 1¼lbs cockles, well
　washed
☐ 12 small clams, well washed
☐ 3 tbsps butter
☐ 1lb 6oz long grain rice
☐ 1¼ cups heavy cream
☐ Fresh herbs (chervil)
☐ Salt and pepper

1 Peel and slice the shallots crosswise. Trim, wash and slice the mushrooms finely.

2 In a frying pan, cook the shallots with the clams and the white wine, covered, until the clams open.

3 Remove the clams. Leave the liquid in the pan. Add the mussels and cook, covered, until the shells open.

4 Meanwhile, trim, wash, dry and finely chop the leaves of the parsley. Set aside.

5 Remove the mussels from the frying pan when opened, and cook the cockles in the same liquid, covered, until they open.

9 In a frying pan, heat the butter and fry together the shellfish, mushrooms and the rice, shaking the pan continuously. Cook for 2 minutes over a high heat.

6 Remove the opened cockles and cook the small clams, covered, in the same liquid until open.

10 Pour into the frying pan water or fish stock equal to $1\frac{1}{2}$ times the volume of the rice. Season, cover and cook in hot oven 425^{0}F for 25 minutes.

7 Remove the shellfish from the shells. Cut out the intestinal bags from the larger fish, if necessary. Rinse well to eliminate sand.

11 Reduce the cooking liquid from the shellfish for 1 minute over a medium heat. Add the cream and reduce for 2 minutes more. Blend the mixture smooth and add the parsley.

8 Strain the cooking liquid through a cheesecloth-lined sieve, discard the impurities and set aside the stock.

12 Serve the rice and the shellfish in a mound with the sauce poured around the edge. Garnish with the chervil.

SALT COD

WITH

PEPPERS

SERVES : 6

PREPARATION TIME : 50 Minutes
COOKING TIME : 1 Hour 20 Minutes
SOAKING TIME : 24 Hours

This dish is based on a traditional Portuguese country recipe using potato, cod and tomato. It has been modernized and refined in an elegant preparation of layered puréed potato, cod and ratatouille.

INGREDIENTS

- [ ] 2lbs salt cod
- [ ] 4 peppers (2 red, 2 green)
- [ ] 3 large onions
- [ ] 6 cloves garlic
- [ ] 1 small red chili pepper
- [ ] 5 large potatoes
- [ ] 3 tbsps olive oil
- [ ] 4 tbsps heavy cream
- [ ] 2 tbsps chopped parsley
- [ ] 2 tomatoes, peeled, seeded and chopped
- [ ] Fresh herbs (chervil)
- [ ] Salt and pepper

1 Cut the salt cod into pieces. Soak in water for 24 hours, changing the water several times.

2 Cut open the peppers, remove the seeds and white pith. Slice.

3 Peel and chop the onions finely. Cut the garlic cloves in half and remove the central shoot. Chop the garlic. Seed and chop the chili pepper.

4 Peel the potatoes. Quarter them and cook in boiling salted water with 1 chopped onion and 1 tbsp of olive oil for 30 minutes.

5

Drain the potatoes and onions when cooled. Blend smooth or press through a sieve. Add the cream and parsley, and season to taste.

9

Add the peppers and the two remaining onions. Cook for 10 minutes over a moderate heat, stirring well.

6

Bring to a boil the soaked and drained cod in a large quantity of water and cook for 5 minutes.

10

Add the tomato to the peppers and onions, and cook for another 15 minutes, stirring frequently. Season to taste.

7

Set aside to drain and cool. Flake with your fingers, discarding the skin and bones.

11

Oil the bottom of an ovenproof pan. Arrange a layer of the potato purée over the bottom. Spread over the cod.

8

Fry the chopped garlic and chili pepper in 3¹/₂ tbsp oil until soft and lightly colored.

12

Top with a layer of the pepper, onion and tomato mixture. Bake in a hot oven 400°F for 30 minutes. Serve hot, garnished with the chopped chervil.

MINUTE SALMON

WITH

VANILLA

VINAIGRETTE

SERVES : 6

PREPARATION TIME : 30 Minutes
COOKING TIME : 15 Minutes

An unusual and surprisingly tasty flavor combination ; quickly sautéed, thinly sliced salmon and cooked green beans are served with a vanilla vinaigrette. This dish can be served as a first course or as a cold main course.

INGREDIENTS

- ☐ 1 salmon (2½ lbs approximately)
- ☐ 1 lb green beans
- ☐ 2 shallots
- ☐ ½ vanilla bean
- ☐ 1 tbsp wine vinegar
- ☐ 4 tbsps oil
- ☐ 1 bunch chives
- ☐ Fresh dill
- ☐ 1 egg
- ☐ 2 tbsps olive oil
- ☐ 1 tbsp butter
- ☐ Salt and pepper

1 Fillet the salmon using a sharp knife. Remove any bones with a vegetable peeler.

2 Cut each strip of salmon into 3 pieces, slicing at an angle.

3 Wash and trim the green beans. Cook in boiling, salted water for 8 to 10 minutes.

4 Drain, then rinse the beans. Slice them into very thin strips.

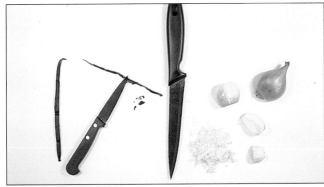

5 Peel the shallots, cut them in two, lengthwise, then chop finely. Cut open the vanilla bean and remove the seeds by scraping with the back of a knife.

6 To make the sauce, mix together the salt, pepper, and vinegar. Allow to dissolve then add the vanilla seeds and shallots. Whisk in the oil.

7 Chop the chives finely. Trim and chop the dill leaves. Set aside.

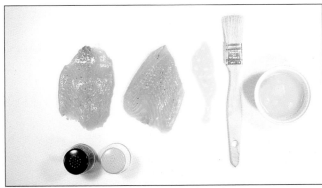

8 Beat the egg in a ramekin and brush the salmon pieces on both sides. Season.

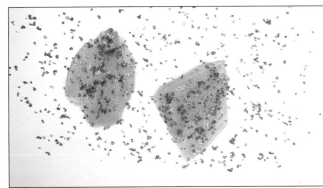

9 Sprinkle the salmon with the chopped chives (reserving some for presentation), and season again.

10 Heat the olive oil in a frying pan and add the butter. When the butter is bubbling, sear the fish for 40 seconds on each side.

11 Mix the green beans in a bowl with the vinaigrette dressing.

12 Drain the lightly cooked salmon on kitchen paper. Serve immediately with the green beans and vinaigrette. Garnish with the chopped herbs (dill and chives).

SEA SCALLOPS À LA NAGE

WITH LEEKS

AND TRUFFLES

SERVES : 6

PREPARATION TIME : 35 Minutes
COOKING TIME : 20 Minutes

*A rich and expensive dish which deserves
special occasions. Fresh sea scallops swim in a
thin cream sauce with sautéed leeks and sliced
black truffles. The costly truffles, found in
specialty food shops, can be reduced in quantity
or eliminated, since there is no substitute.*

INGREDIENTS

- ☐ 18 sea scallops in their shells
- ☐ 3 medium leeks
- ☐ 2 tbsps butter
- ☐ 1¼ cup fish stock
- ☐ 2 truffles, brushed clean
- ☐ 1 cup heavy cream
- ☐ Fresh herbs (chervil, chives)
- ☐ Salt and pepper

1 Open the scallops with the tip of a sharp knife, prising off the top shell.

2 When open, slip the knife in under the scallop and cut it out from the shell.

3 Remove the fleshy, "bearded" parts from around the scallop. Discard. Save the coral for another dish.

4 Rinse the scallops, removing all sand. Dry on a kitchen towel.

5 Cut the roots off the leeks. Cut them in 4 lengthwise. Wash carefully and shred finely.

9 Cut the truffles into even-sized rounds and then into very thin matchstick slices.

6 Melt the butter in a deep saucepan and add the leek. Cook, stirring, for 1 minute.

10 Add the cream, truffles and truffle juice to the leeks and scallops. Cook for 5 minutes.

7 Pour over the stock, season with salt and pepper and cook on a simmer for 15 minutes.

11 Meanwhile, wash and dry the chives and the chervil leaves. Chop finely.

8 Slice the scallops crosswise in 2 or 3 pieces and add them to the saucepan. Cook 1 minute.

12 Serve the scallops and sauce hot, garnished with the chopped herbs.

MILLEFEUILLE

OF SALMON

WITH

FENNEL

SERVES : 6

PREPARATION TIME : 1 Hour
COOKING TIME : 45 Minutes

Millefeuille, or "thousand leaves", is usually associated with a flaky pastry dessert. In this case it refers to a multi-layered dish of thinly sliced salmon and sliced cooked fennel. The light sauce is a reduction of fish stock and fennel juice.

INGREDIENTS

- ☐ 1 carrot
- ☐ ½ leek
- ☐ 2 shallots
- ☐ 1 onion
- ☐ 2 tbsps olive oil
- ☐ 2lbs fish bones and trimmings
- ☐ 4 fennel bulbs
- ☐ Juice of 1 lemon
- ☐ 1½ cups heavy cream
- ☐ 2lbs salmon fillets
- ☐ ½ bunch chives
- ☐ Salt and pepper

1 Peel, wash and chop the carrot, leek, shallots and onion.

2 In a casserole, heat the oil and add the chopped vegetables. Add the fish bones and trimmings, and sauté for 5 minutes.

3 Add water to cover, with 1 tsp salt and boil for 20 minutes. Skim the top of the water from time to time.

4 Trim the fennel and chop two of the bulbs very finely. Use a food processor, if available.

5 Cook the fennel for 3 minutes in boiling, salted water with the lemon juice. Drain and refresh in cold water.

6 Place the fennel in a saucepan with half the cream, season, cover and cook gently for 10 minutes.

7 Cut the salmon into thin slices with a serrated knife. Season.

8 In 6 metal rings (on wax paper) or greased ramekins layer the salmon with the fennel mixture.

9 Place the two remaining fennel bulbs in a juice extractor, or blend in a food processor and strain the juice. Reserve the juice.

10 Strain the fish stock through a fine sieve lined with cheesecloth. Measure off 1 cup. Cook the salmon millefeuilles in a hot oven 400ºF for 10 minutes.

11 Reduce the stock by half, add the remaining cream, and boil for 2 minutes. Add the fennel juice at the last moment. Blend smooth with a hand held electric blender. Season.

12 Run a knife around the sides of the salmon millefeuilles, turn out and serve with the sauce. Sprinkle with the chopped chives.

OCEAN PERCH

AND

JUMBO SHRIMP
DUET

SERVES : 6

PREPARATION TIME : 30 Minutes
COOKING TIME : 35 Minutes

*Ratatouille vegetables of onion, eggplant,
zucchini and tomato are slowly cooked, then
puréed, and topped with steamed fish and
jumbo shrimp sautéed in olive oil. This tasty fish
dish is elegant, yet low in calories.*

INGREDIENTS

- ☐ 18 raw jumbo shrimp
- ☐ 2lbs ocean perch fillets
- ☐ 1 pepper (½ red and ½ green)
- ☐ 1 onion
- ☐ 1 tomato, peeled and seeded
- ☐ 1 zucchini
- ☐ 5 tbsps olive oil
- ☐ 1 clove garlic
- ☐ Bouquet garni (parsley, thyme, bay leaf)
- ☐ 1⅛ cups fish stock
- ☐ Fresh herbs (chervil)
- ☐ Salt and pepper

1 Peel the shrimp and remove their heads and tails.

2 Cut down the back of the shrimp, devein them and cut them in two, lengthwise.

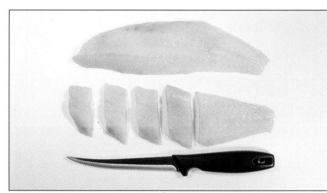

3 Cut the perch fillets into even, bite-sized pieces.

4 Remove the pith and seeds from the peppers and slice them thinly. Peel and chop the onion finely.

5 Chop the tomato to obtain a pulp. Cut the garlic in half, and remove the central shoot.

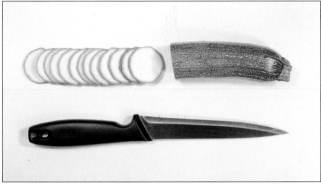

6 Trim the ends of the zucchini, wash and cut into thin rounds.

7 In 3 tbsps of olive oil, fry the onion and the peppers for 3 minutes. Add the garlic, zucchini and the tomato pulp. Mix well.

8 After frying for 5 minutes, add the bouquet garni, salt, pepper and the fish stock. Cover and cook over a moderate heat for 20 minutes, stirring frequently.

9 Heat 2 tbsps of olive oil and sear the shrimp evenly all over for 3 minutes. Season with salt and pepper. Drain on paper towels and keep warm in the oven.

10 Place the fish fillets in a steamer. Season with salt and pepper, and cook, covered, for 5 minutes.

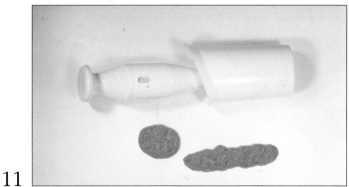

11 Remove the bouquet garni from the vegetable mixture and blend to a smooth purée with a hand-held electric blender.

12 Serve the fish fillets and shrimp with the vegetable purée sauce, and garnished with the fresh herbs (chervil).

RED SNAPPER

WITH

NUTMEG

SERVES : 6

PREPARATION TIME : 1 Hour
COOKING TIME : 50 Minutes

*For this original fish dish, zucchini "galettes"
are prepared much like potato pancakes, then
decoratively topped with sautéed fish fillets and
served in a nutmeg-flavored cream sauce.*

INGREDIENTS

- ☐ 2 red snappers (2¹/₂lbs each)
- ☐ 8 zucchinis
- ☐ 1 egg
- ☐ 1 tbsp crème fraîche or sour cream
- ☐ 5 tbsps olive oil
- ☐ ¹/₂ cup rich fish stock
- ☐ 1¹/₂ cups heavy cream
- ☐ 1 nutmeg
- ☐ ¹/₂ lemon
- ☐ 2 tbsps butter
- ☐ ¹/₂ bunch chives, chopped
- ☐ Salt and pepper

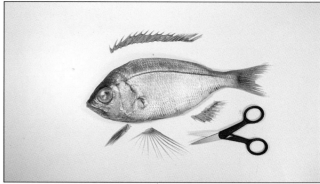

1 Cut the fins off the red snapper with a pair of scissors.

2 Scrape off the scales with a fish scaler or the blade of a sharp knife. Gut and rinse well.

3 With a sharp knife, cut off the fillets, running the knife carefully down the backbone.

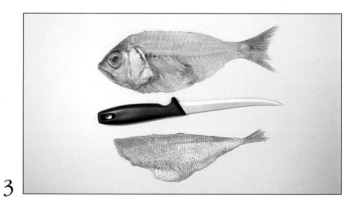

4 Using a vegetable grater, slice the zucchini into thin julienne. Discard the soft seed centre.

5 In a bowl, beat the eggs with the crème fraîche, salt, and pepper and then add the zucchini. Mix thoroughly with a fork.

6 In a small ovenproof frying pan, heat 1 tbsp of oil and fry ⅓ of the zucchini mixture, flattening it into a pancake shape.

7 After about 3 minutes turn over the zucchini galette and finish cooking it in a hot oven 400°F. Repeat the process three times.

8 Reduce the stock by half, then stir in the heavy cream, 6 or 7 scrapings of nutmeg, salt and pepper. Boil for 1 minute.

9 Remove from the heat, blend smooth with a hand held electric blender, add a few drops of lemon juice and keep warm in a bowl of hot water.

10 Season the red snapper fillets with salt and pepper and a few scrapings of nutmeg.

11 In 2 tbsps of oil melt the butter and fry the red snapper fillets on both sides until lightly. Finish cooking in a hot oven 400°F for 8 minutes.

12 Cut the galettes into 8 pieces, spread the pieces out on a plate, lay the fillets over and pour over the sauce. Sprinkle on the chopped chives.

GRILLED SEA BASS

WITH

FENNEL

AND ANISEED

SERVES : 6

PREPARATION TIME : 40 Minutes
COOKING TIME : 30 Minutes
MARINADE : 1 Hour

Fennel, an aniseed-flavored plant of Italian origin, is sautéed in butter and served with grilled fish fillets. It is topped with a puréed and lightly creamed tomato and shallot sauce and garnished with fresh dill.

GRILLED SEA BASS WITH FENNEL AND ANISEED

INGREDIENTS

- [ ] 6 small sea bass
- [ ] Juice of ½ lemon
- [ ] 1 tbsp anise seed
- [ ] 3 tbsps olive oil
- [ ] 3 fennel bulbs
- [ ] 2 cups milk
- [ ] 2 shallots
- [ ] 2 tomatoes
- [ ] 1½ cups rich fish stock
- [ ] 1 cup heavy cream
- [ ] 2 tbsps butter
- [ ] Fresh herbs (dill)
- [ ] Salt and pepper

1 Scale and gut the sea bass. Remove the fillets by cutting down the backbone.

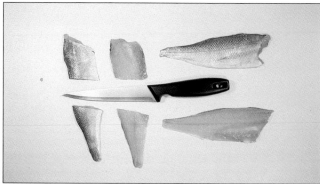

2 Cut each of the fillets in two, to obtain 4 small fillets per person. Season with salt and pepper.

3 Mix together the lemon juice, aniseed and 2 tbsps olive oil. Add the fish fillets, and marinate for 1 hour, turning from time to time.

4 Wash, trim and slice the fennel. Discard the hard center core.

5 Bring the milk to a boil. Add salt and the fennel slices and cook for 5 minutes. Drain, then spread to dry on a kitchen towel.

9 Strain this sauce through a fine sieve, pushing through with a spoon to obtain a smooth sauce. Keep warm over boiling water Preheat a cast-iron griddle and grease it with a little oil.

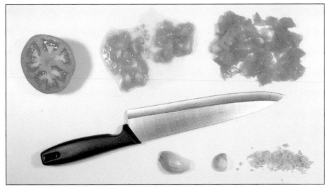

6 Peel and finely chop the shallot. Cut the tomatoes in half, squeeze to extract the pips. Chop roughly.

10 Sear the fish fillets on each side, beginning skin side down. Place in an ovenproof pan and finish cooking in a hot oven 400°F for 10 minutes.

7 Drain the marinade into a frying pan Add the shallots and tomato. Heat for 3 minutes, then add the fish stock. Reduce on a high heat for 5 minutes.

11 Sauté the fennel in the remaining butter until lightly colored. Season with salt and pepper.

8 When reduced, add the cream and bring to a boil. Remove from the heat and blend smooth with a hand held electric blender. Check seasoning.

12 Remove the fish from the oven. To serve, Top the fennel with the fish and the sauce. Garnish with fresh dill.

ROLLED FILLET
OF SOLE

WITH

BELGIAN ENDIVE

SERVES : 6

PREPARATION TIME : 1 Hour
COOKING TIME : 20 Minutes

*A wonderful taste combination, flattened sole
fillets are filled with sliced bacon, rolled, then
steamed. They are served with sautéed endive
and a lightly flavored cream sauce.*

INGREDIENTS

☐ 3 sole
☐ 12 thin slices bacon
☐ 6 heads of Belgian endive
☐ 1½ cups heavy cream
☐ 3 tbsps butter
☐ Fresh herbs (dill)
☐ Salt and pepper

1 Pull the skins (white and black) off the sole. Use a cloth to help you hold the fish firmly.

2 Using a flexible knife, cut along the backbone and remove the fillets.

3 When you have removed the fillets, wrap them in plastic wrap and press flat with the blade of a large chopping knife.

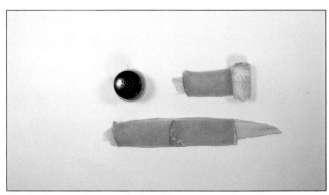

4 Cut the bacon slices to fit the fillets exactly. Save the trimmings. Season with pepper. Roll up neatly and tightly.

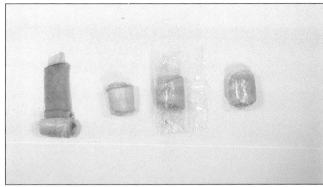

5 Place each roll on a piece of plastic wrap. Fold it up and over the rolled fillets, twisting the two ends to close.

6 Separate all the endive leaves, wash, dry and cut in fine julienne, with a stainless-steel knife.

7 Bring the blender to a boil. Blend smooth with a hand-held electric blender, then add the bacon trimmings sliced finely. Keep warm over hot water.

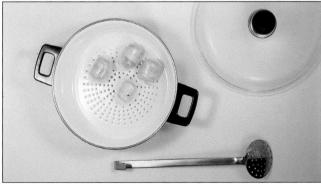

8 Cook the rolled fillets in a steamer for 10 minutes.

9 Heat the butter in a pan. When foaming, sauté the endive over a high heat. It may be necessary to cook it in two batches.

10 Season the endive with salt and pepper. When cooked (approximately 3 minutes), set aside.

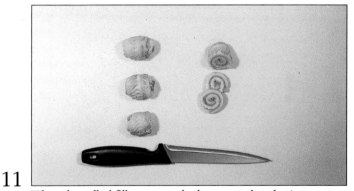

11 When the rolled fillets are cooked, remove the plastic wrap and slice into round slices.

12 Place the slices on a bed of endive with the reheated sauce. Sprinkle with chopped herbs (dill) and serve.

MARINATED RAW FISH

SERVES : 6

PREPARATION TIME : 40 Minutes
MARINADE : 10 Minutes

*This makes a lovely light entrée to any meal.
Thinly sliced salmon and whitefish fillets are
"cooked" in a lemon juice and olive oil
marinade flavored with shallot and pepper and
served with sliced vegetables. It is essential to this
recipe that the fish, of whatever variety, be
exceptionally fresh.*

INGREDIENTS

☐ ¹/₂ small salmon (approximately 1lb 8oz), halved lengthwise
☐ 1 fillet ocean perch or whitefish (approximately 12oz)
☐ 1 carrot
☐ ¹/₂ cucumber
☐ 1 stick celery
☐ 2 shallots
☐ 2 sprigs dill
☐ 1 curly endive
☐ 2 lemons
☐ Mixed peppercorns in a pepper mill
☐ 4 tbsps olive oil
☐ 1 small jar lumpfish caviar
☐ Salt and pepper

1 Slice the salmon very thinly with a sharp, serrated knife.

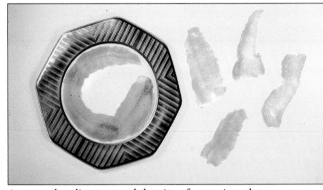

2 Arrange the slices around the rim of a serving platter, overlapping them.

3 Cut smaller slices of the ocean perch, proceeding as in step 1.

4 Interlace the perch slices with the salmon, working towards the center of the platter.

5 Peel and cut the carrot into thin slices. Cut the slices into very thin julienne strips.

6 Cut the cucumber into chunks. Peel thickly, using a sharp knife. Discard the core. Cut the peel into julienne.

7 Peel the celery. Cut thin, even slices with a vegetable peeler. Cut into julienne.

8 Peel the shallots and halve them lengthwise. Finely and evenly chop the halves.

9 Wash and trim the curly endive and the dill. Discard the stalks of the dill and finely chop the leaves.

10 Squeeze the two lemons and mix the juice with the shallots and dill leaves.

11 Season the lemon juice and dill mixture with salt and a few turns of the pepper mill. Whisk in the olive oil.

12 Brush the sauce over all the fish. Marinate for 10 minutes and serve with the salad and julienned vegetables tossed in the remaining sauce. Garnish with the lumpfish caviar.

RED SNAPPER

WITH

CELERY

AND CELERIAC

SERVES : 6

PREPARATION TIME : 40 Minutes
COOKING TIME : 20 Minutes

*Use a whole fish to carry out this recipe
correctly, since the liver is used to flavor the
sauce. The fillets are sautéed in butter with
parsley, and served with celery and celeriac.
If using bought fillets, simply eliminate the liver
flavoring for the celery sauce.*

INGREDIENTS

- ☐ 12 small red snapper
- ☐ ½ large head celeriac
- ☐ 3 sticks celery
- ☐ 3 tbsps parsley
- ☐ ½ egg, beaten
- ☐ ¾ cup rich fish stock
- ☐ ¾ cup heavy cream
- ☐ 2 tbsps butter
- ☐ 2 tbsps olive oil
- ☐ Fresh herbs (chervil)
- ☐ Salt and pepper

1 Scale, gut and rinse the snapper. Remove the fillets, running the knife down the backbone.

2 Remove the livers from the snapper heads. Discard the bones and trimmings.

3 Peel the celeriac and cut into thin slices. Cut the slices into thin strips. Cut the celery sticks into slices.

4 Wash and dry the parsley, chop it very finely.

5 Season each fillet with salt and pepper, and brush the flesh side with beaten egg.

6 Dredge the side of fish covered with egg in the chopped parsley, so the parsley adheres.

7 Bring the fish stock to a boil with the livers and parsley trimmings. Boil for 2 minutes, then remove from the heat.

8 Add 2 sticks of chopped celery to the fish stock and process in a food processor. Season lightly with salt and pepper.

9 Strain the sauce through a cheesecloth-lined sieve into a saucepan, pushing the mixture through. Add the cream and cook gently for 5 minutes. Set aside.

10 Butter a square of wax paper and spread the remaining celery and the celeriac on it. Season well with salt and pepper. Cook in a steam-cooker for 5 minutes.

11 Sear the fish fillets in hot oil, skin-side down first, then turn and sear the other side. Cook each side 2 to 3 minutes.

12 Serve the cooked celery topped with the fillets, and the hot sauce, blended a second time. Garnish with fresh herbs (chervil).

STUFFED GAME HENS

WITH

GRAPES

SERVES : 8

PREPARATION TIME : 1 Hour 30 Minutes
COOKING TIME : 1 Hour 15 Minutes

Game hens are first boned, then stuffed with a mixture of ground turkey breast, bread, milk and herbs, and then baked. They are served with a sauce made with fresh pressed grapes and chicken stock thickened with butter. Accompany with sautéed onion and zucchini.

INGREDIENTS

- [ ] 2 young game hens
- [ ] 12oz turkey breast
- [ ] ¹/₂ egg, beaten
- [ ] 2 shallots
- [ ] 1 tbsp chopped parsley
- [ ] 4oz bread
- [ ] ¹/₂ cup milk
- [ ] 2 tbsps cream
- [ ] 1 carrot
- [ ] 1 onion
- [ ] ¹/₄ stick celery
- [ ] 5 tbsps oil
- [ ] 2 tbsps Muscat wine
- [ ] 1 bouquet garni (parsley, thyme, bay leaf)
- [ ] 4 tbsps butter
- [ ] 1 onion, chopped
- [ ] 5 medium zucchini
- [ ] 8oz grapes
- [ ] Fresh herbs (chervil)
- [ ] Salt and pepper

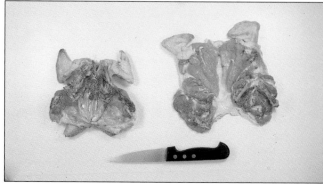

1 Bone the game hens, cutting along the breast bone to begin. Remove all the meat from the carcass. Reserve the carcasses.

2 Mix together in a food processor the turkey breast, egg, shallots and bread (presoaked in milk), and process for 1 minute. Add the cream and season with salt and pepper.

3 Chop the carrot, onion and celery quite finely.

4 Sear the carcasses in 2 tbsps oil with the above vegetables. When the ingredients are lightly colored, deglaze with the Muscat wine.

5 Pour in 1 cup water, season and add the bouquet garni. Reduce over high heat for 15 minutes.

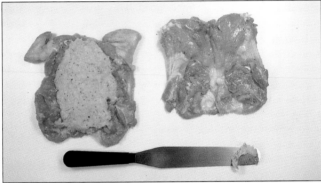

6 Spread the stuffing down the length of the game hens using a spatula.

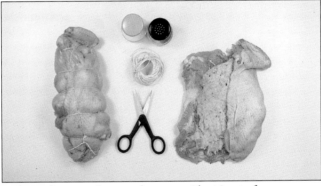

7 Reshape the game hens and secure with string to form 2 sausage shapes. Season the skin side with salt and pepper.

8 Sear the stuffed game hens in 1 tbsp oil until lightly browned. Finish cooking in a hot oven 400°F for 40 minutes, turning frequently.

9 In a large frying pan, heat 2 tbsps oil with 2 tbsp butter and sauté the onion and zucchini until lightly colored, and cooked through. Season to taste.

10 In a juice extractor, process ³/₄ of the grapes to obtain 1 cup juice. Cut the remaining grapes in half, and reserve for the sauce.

11 Strain the cooking juices from the game hens through a sieve to obtain ³/₄ cup liquid. Reduce in a casserole with the grape juice, by ¹/₃. Mix in the remaining butter.

12 When cooked, slice the game hens and serve with the sautéed onion and zucchini. Garnish with the sauce seasoned to taste, the reserved grape halves and fresh chervil.

CARAMELIZED CHICKEN WINGS

SERVES : 6

PREPARATION TIME : 30 Minutes
COOKING TIME : 50 Minutes

*An economical dish full of flavor, chicken wings
are oven-baked in a garlic, vinegar and honey
sauce until lightly caramelized and served with
fresh sautéed bean sprouts. The chicken wings
are also good served with drinks.*

INGREDIENTS

- ☐ 5 slices fresh ginger root
- ☐ 1 clove garlic
- ☐ 18 chicken wings
- ☐ 3 tbsps honey
- ☐ 5 tbsps soy sauce
- ☐ 2 tbsps vinegar
- ☐ 1 sprig thyme
- ☐ 2 bay leaves
- ☐ 1lb fresh bean sprouts
- ☐ 1 tsp sesame oil
- ☐ 1 tsp sugar
- ☐ ½ bunch chives
- ☐ 10 mint leaves
- ☐ 1 tomato
- ☐ Salt and pepper

1 Peel the ginger and chop finely. Discard the central shoot from the garlic and chop the rest finely.

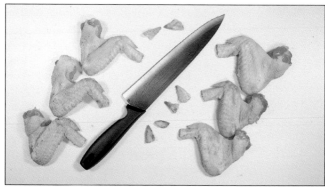

2 Trim the wing-tips off the chicken wings.

3 In a bowl, mix together the honey, 4 tbsps soy sauce, the garlic, ginger, 1 tbsp vinegar and 1 tbsp water.

4 In a saucepan of water, bring to a boil the chicken wings with the thyme and bay leaves. Remove and drain the wings.

5 Arrange the wings in an ovenproof dish, and pour over the honey-soy sauce mixture. Cook in a hot oven 400°F for 40 minutes.

9 Add 1 tbsp soy sauce, 1 tbsp vinegar and the sugar to the bean sprouts after they have cooked. Cook for 2 minutes more, shaking the pan. Remove from heat.

6 Wash and drain the bean sprouts ; dry on a kitchen towel.

10 Chop the chives. Cut the mint leaves into thin strips.

7 Sauté the bean sprouts in the sesame oil for 5 minutes, stirring frequently.

11 Cube only the flesh part of the tomato, discarding the seeds and juice.

8 Turn the chicken wings frequently as they cook, to ensure even caramelizing.

12 Serve the caramelized chicken wings on top of the bean sprouts ; garnish with herbs (chives and mint) and the cubes of tomato.

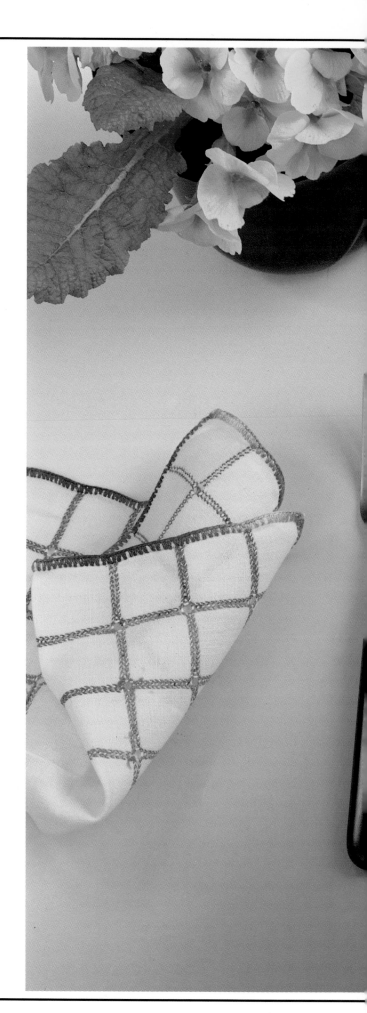

YOGURT MARINATED CHICKEN

SERVES : 6

PREPARATION TIME : 20 Minutes
COOKING TIME : 1 Hour 20 Minutes
MARINADE : 24 Hours

*A variation on Indian tandoori chicken.
Chicken pieces are marinated in a spicy yogurt
mixture overnight, then slowly cooked on a grill.
They are served with saffron-flavored rice.*

INGREDIENTS

- ☐ 1 chicken
- ☐ 2 cardamom pods
- ☐ 1½ cups yogurt
- ☐ ½ cup milk
- ☐ 1 tsp curry powder
- ☐ 1 tsp turmeric
- ☐ ½ tsp cinnamon
- ☐ 5 tbsps olive oil
- ☐ 1 onion, chopped
- ☐ ½ small red chili pepper
- ☐ 1½ cups basmati rice
- ☐ 2 cups chicken stock
- ☐ A good pinch saffron
- ☐ 5 sprigs coriander
- ☐ Salt and pepper

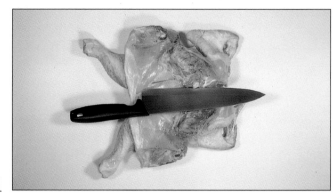

1 Cut the chicken in half by slicing down along the backbone. Open the chicken out flat.

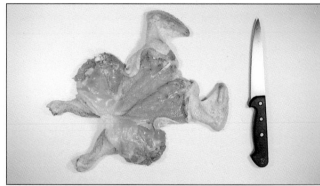

2 Cut away the flesh from the bones by running a sharp-bladed knife between the flesh and the bones.

3 Open up the cardamom pods, extract the seeds and chop them finely.

4 In a bowl, whisk together the yogurt, milk and spices (curry powder, cardamon, turmeric, cinnamon), salt and pepper.

5 Place the flattened chicken in a glass baking pan, pour over the marinade and leave overnight in the refrigerator, turning frequently.

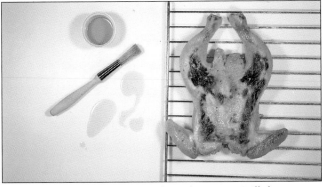

6 The next day, drain the marinade and reserve. Grill the chicken or roast in the oven, brushing it with 2 tbsps olive oil during the cooking. Turn the chicken often.

7 Heat 3 tbsps of oil and fry the onions for 1 minute. Add the chili pepper. Add the rice to the onions. Preheat the oven to 400°F.

8 Mix the rice and onions, then pour over the chicken stock, flavored with the saffron. Season, cover and cook for 20 minutes in the preheated oven. Remove the chili pepper.

9 Turn the chicken frequently during cooking. Heat the marinade in a saucepan over a low heat, stirring gently.

10 Wash, dry and finely chop the leafy part of the coriander. Set aside for the sauce.

11 When the chicken is cooked (approximately 1 hour), remove from the oven and cut into quarters.

12 Serve the chicken pieces with the hot marinade sauce, the chopped coriander and the saffron rice.

CHICKEN SUPRÊME

WITH

ASPARAGUS

SERVES : 6

PREPARATION TIME : 40 Minutes
COOKING TIME : 1 Hour

*A lovely taste combination; chicken breasts are
first coated in chopped fresh tarragon, then
sautéed in butter and served with steamed
asparagus. The delicate sauce consists of the
asparagus juices enriched with cream and
flavored with tarragon.*

INGREDIENTS

- ☐ 1lb asparagus
- ☐ 6 cups chicken stock
- ☐ 1 bunch fresh tarragon
- ☐ 6 chicken breasts
- ☐ 1 egg, beaten
- ☐ ½ cup heavy cream
- ☐ 2 tbsps oil
- ☐ 1 tbsp butter
- ☐ Salt and pepper

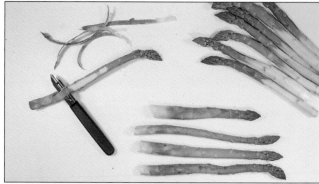

1 Peel the asparagus with a vegetable peeler. It is not necessary to trim the tips.

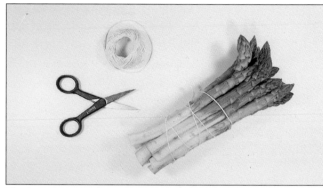

2 Tie the asparagus into a neat bunch with kitchen string.

3 Stand the bunches, tips uppermost and cook in the boiling stock for 4 minutes (since the roots are tougher than the tips).

4 After 4 minutes, cook the asparagus horizontally for another 10 to 15 minutes. Remove and drain. Reserve the stock.

5 Cut off the leafy part of the tarragon. Chop finely. Add the stalks to the stock and boil for 15 minutes.

9 Remove the tarragon stalks from the stock. In a food processor, blend 1 cup of the stock and the asparagus stalks smooth. Strain the sauce through a fine sieve.

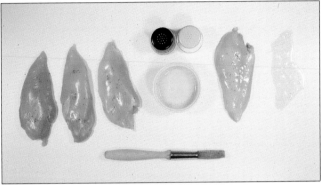

6 Meanwhile, season the chicken breasts and brush completely with the beaten egg.

10 Add almost all the remaining tarragon to the sauce. Add the cream and bring to a boil. Blend smooth again. Season.

7 Coat both sides of the breasts with $1/2$ of the chopped tarragon.

11 Heat the oil and butter together and sear the chicken breasts on each side. Finish cooking, uncovered, in a moderate oven 350°F for 20 minutes.

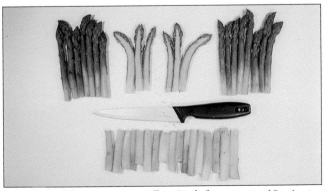

8 Cut off $1/3$ of the asparagus stalks. Cook for an extra 10 minutes in the stock. Set aside. Cut the tips in two, lengthwise.

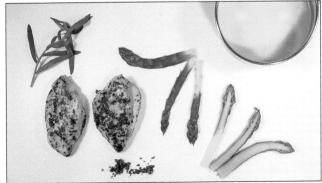

12 Serve the chicken breasts and the asparagus tips with the sauce. Garnish with chopped tarragon.

TURKEY FILLET STUFFED

WITH

CHEESE

SERVES : 6

PREPARATION TIME : 50 Minutes
COOKING TIME : 35 Minutes

An elegant yet simple preparation of turkey breasts ; thinly sliced and rolled with ham and cheese. The dish is cooked on top of the stove or baked in the oven. Serve with tomato halves baked with garlic and parsley.

INGREDIENTS

- ☐ 1³/₄ lbs turkey breast
- ☐ 4oz Gruyère or Swiss cheese
- ☐ ½ bunch chives
- ☐ 6 slices Parma ham
- ☐ 2 eggs
- ☐ 6 slices bread
- ☐ 6 tomatoes
- ☐ 1 tbsp chopped parsley
- ☐ 1 clove garlic (central shoot removed)
- ☐ 2 tbsps olive oil
- ☐ 3 tbsps oil
- ☐ 2 tbsps butter
- ☐ Fresh herbs (chervil)
- ☐ Salt and pepper

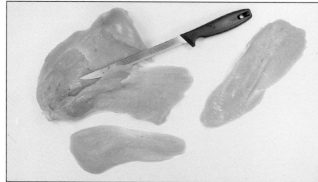

1 Cut the turkey breast into 6 long, thin scallops.

2 Slice the cheese thinly. Chop the chives.

3 Sprinkle the chives over the cheese slices and arrange the cheese slices on the slices of ham. Roll up.

4 Cover the turkey slices with plastic wrap and, using the flat side of a cleaver, pound them flat.

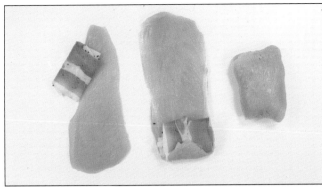

5

Place the ham and cheese rolls on the flattened turkey slices and roll up.

6

Beat the egg, and dip the rolls in it so that they are well coated. Season with salt and pepper.

7

Process the slices of bread to form breadcrumbs.

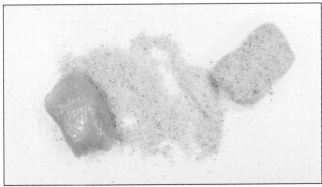

8

Coat the turkey rolls in the breadcrumbs to cover completely.

9

Halve the tomatoes. Chop the parsley and garlic together, and place approximately 1 teaspoon on each tomato half. Sprinkle a few drops of olive oil on each.

10

Arrange the tomatoes in an ovenproof baking pan. Sprinkle over any remaining breadcrumbs. Bake in a hot oven 400°F for 15 minutes.

11

Heat the oil and butter in a frying pan, and sear the turkey rolls on both sides. Cook over a gentle heat, for 15 to 20 minutes or bake in a moderate 350°F oven.

12

Serve the turkey rolls with the tomatoes, garnished with chopped chervil.

DUCK BREAST

WITH

SPICES

SERVES : 6

PREPARATION TIME : 40 Minutes
COOKING TIME : 30 Minutes
MARINADE : 24 Hours

Duck breast is marinated for several hours or overnight in an exotic mixture of honey, soy sauce and spices. It is browned, baked and served thinly sliced with a decorative rosette of cooked tomatoes and zucchini.

INGREDIENTS

- ☐ 3 duck breasts
- ☐ 5 slices fresh ginger root, peeled
- ☐ 2 tbsps honey
- ☐ ½ tsp curry powder
- ☐ ½ tsp turmeric
- ☐ Pinch of cinnamon
- ☐ 8 tbsps soy sauce
- ☐ 3 firm tomatoes
- ☐ 1 large zucchini
- ☐ 3 tbsps olive oil
- ☐ 1 sprig dried thyme
- ☐ 1 tbsp sugar
- ☐ 2 tbsps vinegar
- ☐ ½ clove garlic (central shoot removed and finely chopped)
- ☐ 6 tbsps water
- ☐ 1 tbsp chopped chives
- ☐ Salt and pepper

1 The day before, prepare the marinade. Slit the duck breasts using the point of a small knife, season on each side with salt and pepper.

2 Chop the ginger finely.

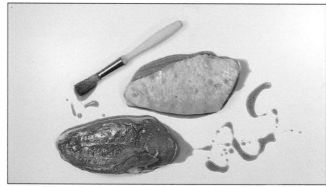

3 In a bowl, mix together the honey, curry powder, turmeric, cinnamon, ginger and 3 tbsps soy sauce.

4 Brush this syrup mixture over the duck breasts and leave to marinate for 24 hours. Reserve the marinade.

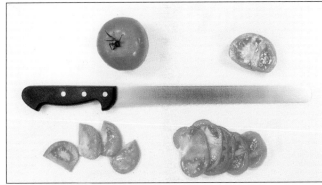

5 Slice the tomatoes thinly with a serrated knife.

6 Cut the zucchini into thin rounds with a sharp knife or a vegetable slicer.

7 Plunge the zucchini into boiling, salted water for 1 minute. Drain and dry on a tea towel.

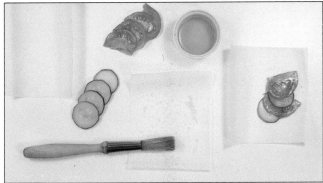

8 Oil squares of wax paper and interlace the tomato and zucchini slices to form rose shapes.

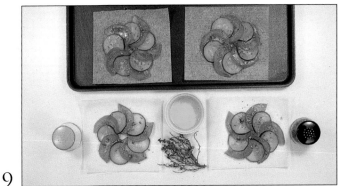

9 Season the vegetable rosettes with salt and pepper, brush lightly with olive oil and sprinkle with thyme. Just before serving, cook 10 minutes in a hot oven 400°F.

10 In a frying pan, sear the duck breasts in 2 tbsps oil, beginning skin side down and turning after 1 minute. Finish cooking in a hot oven 400°F for 10 to 15 minutes.

11 In a saucepan, mix together the sugar, vinegar, garlic, 5 tbsps soy sauce and 6 tbsps water. Add the reserved marinade. Bring to a boil, then remove from the heat.

12 Cut the breasts into thin slices and serve with the tomato and zucchini rosettes, and a little of the warm sauce. Garnish with chopped chives.

CHICKEN
POT-AU-FEU

WITH

SPICES

SERVES : 4

PREPARATION TIME : 45 Minutes
COOKING TIME : 1 Hour

Based on a traditional French recipe, boiled chicken is modernized with the addition of ginger, cinnamon and cloves. It is served in its stock with croutons and a home-made mayonnaise flavored with diced pickles and parsley.

INGREDIENTS

- ☐ 2 carrots
- ☐ 1 chicken
- ☐ 1 piece fresh ginger root, peeled
- ☐ 1 onion
- ☐ 2 whole cloves
- ☐ Bouquet garni (parsley, thyme, bay leaf)
- ☐ 4 cabbage leaves
- ☐ ½ leek
- ☐ ½ stick cinnamon
- ☐ 5 peppercorns
- ☐ 1 tsp coarse sea salt
- ☐ 1 egg yolk
- ☐ 1 tsp mustard
- ☐ 1 cup oil
- ☐ 10 pickles
- ☐ 1 tbsp chopped parsley
- ☐ ½ French baguette
- ☐ Fresh herbs (chives)
- ☐ Salt and pepper

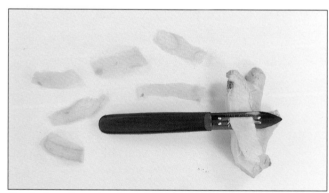

1 Peel and cut the carrots into even-sized matchsticks. Reserve the peelings.

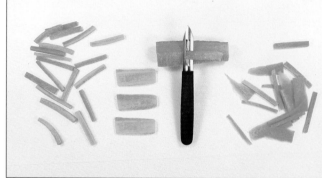

2 Remove the legs and the breasts from the chicken. Break up the carcass.

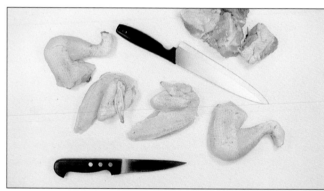

3 Cut 5 slices from the fresh ginger root.

4 Peel the onion, and stud it with the cloves. Tie together the parsley, thyme and bay leaf to form a bouquet garni.

5 In a casserole, cover the chicken and carcass with water. Add the carrot peelings, cabbage, leek and onion. Bring to a boil.

6 When it reaches a boil, skim off the foam. Add the ginger, cinnamon, bouquet garni, peppercorns and sea salt. Cover and cook for 45 minutes.

7 In a bowl, make a mayonnaise by mixing together the egg yolk, mustard, salt and pepper. Gradually whisk in the olive oil.

8 Chop the pickles finely and add them to the mayonnaise along with the parsley. Mix together well and set aside.

9 When the pot-au-feu is cooked, remove the chicken and cabbage. Strain the rest through a fine sieve and return to the heat. Cook the carrot matchsticks for 6 minutes in the stock.

10 Slice the cabbage thinly, and add to the stock along with the chicken, cut into thick slices. Reheat thoroughly.

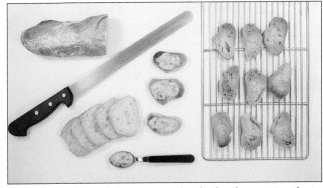

11 Toast slices of French baguette under the broiler, coating the slices with a little mayonnaise.

12 Serve the boiled chicken in shallow bowls with the toasts and garnished with fresh herbs (chives).

CHICKEN ROLLS STUFFED

WITH

CEPS

SERVES : 6

PREPARATION TIME : 1 Hour 30 Minutes
COOKING TIME : 1 Hour

Ceps are a wonderful, meaty wild mushroom found in specialty food shops. For this dish, they are ground with chicken breast, egg and cream and used to stuff boned chicken legs which are rolled, tied and cooked in chicken stock. Slice the rolls to serve and accompany with a galette of potatoes and a cream-enriched sauce.

INGREDIENTS

- ☐ 1oz dried ceps (or other wild mushrooms)
- ☐ 6 chicken legs
- ☐ 1 chicken breast
- ☐ ½ egg, beaten
- ☐ ½ bunch chives
- ☐ 1 tbsp heavy cream
- ☐ 1 piece pork intestine or sausage casing
- ☐ 1lb potatoes
- ☐ ½ onion, chopped
- ☐ 1 tbsp chopped parsley
- ☐ 2 slices pineapple
- ☐ 2 pints chicken stock
- ☐ 2 tbsps oil
- ☐ ½ cup heavy cream
- ☐ Fresh herbs (chives)
- ☐ Salt and pepper

1 Reconstitute the mushrooms in cold water for 1 hour, then chop finely.

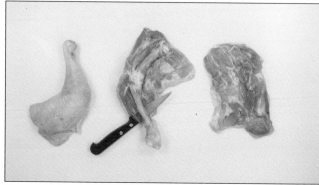

2 Bone the chicken legs by running a sharp knife down and around the bone. Discard the bones.

3 In a food processor, mix together the chicken breast, beaten egg, and the chives. Season well with salt and pepper.

4 Place the meat stuffing in a bowl and mix in half the chopped mushrooms and the 1 tbsp cream.

5 Spread the stuffing down the centers of the boned chicken legs, using a spatula.

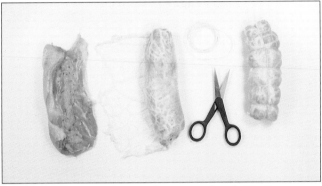

6 Roll up tightly, then place on 6 squares of pork intestine or sausage casing. Roll up and tie with string. Season.

7 Peel and rinse the potatoes. Grate them all.

8 Mix together in a bowl the potato, onion, parsley, salt and pepper. Dice the pineapple and stir it in.

9 Pour the stock into a casserole, add the chicken rolls and simmer for 30 minutes.

10 In a small frying pan, heat the oil and cook thick rounds of the potato mixture to form galettes, browning on each side. Bake in a hot oven 400°F 10 minutes each side.

11 Remove the chicken rolls, and cut the string. Reduce the stock by half. Using a hand-held electric blender, incorporate the cream and remaining mushrooms.

12 Slice the chicken rolls evenly to serve. Accompany with the potato galettes, and the sauce kept warm over hot water. Garnish with chopped chives.

RABBIT STEW
À L'ANCIENNE

SERVES : 6

PREPARATION TIME : 45 Minutes
COOKING TIME : 2 Hours 10 Minutes

This is a recipe for rabbit cooked in the old style ; a traditional stew of rabbit, bacon, onions, and potatoes. The sauce consists of a reduction of the cooking juices.

INGREDIENTS

- ☐ 1 large rabbit
- ☐ 4 cloves garlic (in method)
- ☐ 1 onion
- ☐ 8oz bacon, in one piece
- ☐ Bouquet garni (10 sprigs parsley, thyme, bay leaf)
- ☐ 3 tbsps olive oil
- ☐ 1 cup red wine
- ☐ 1 cup small onions
- ☐ 1 tbsp sugar
- ☐ 1 tbsp butter
- ☐ 12 new potatoes
- ☐ Fresh herbs (chervil)
- ☐ Salt and pepper

1 Chop the rabbit into 12 pieces. Discard the head and the ends of the feet.

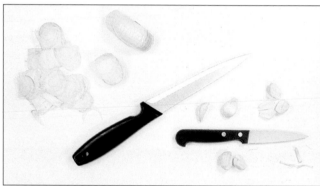

2 Peel the onion and garlic. Remove the central shoot of the garlic. Chop the onion and garlic finely.

3 Remove the bacon rind, slice and then chop the bacon into small rectangles.

4 Make a bouquet garni by tying together the parsley, thyme and bay leaf.

5 In a flameproof casserole, sear the rabbit pieces in the olive oil until lightly browned. Remove from the casserole.

9 Cook the onions in water to cover, with the sugar and butter. Season with salt and pepper. Cook until the water has evaporated, and the sauce is slightly caramelized (approximately 20 minutes).

6 In the same oil, fry the garlic, onion and the bouquet garni. Add the bacon pieces. Allow to color lightly.

10 Peel and trim the potatoes into narrow oblongs.

7 Pour off the excess fat, if necessary. Return the rabbit to the pan and deglaze with the red wine. Add 3 cups water. Cover and cook over a low heat for 1 hour 45 minutes.

11 After the rabbit stew has been cooking for 1 hour 30 minutes, add the potatoes. Cook, covered, until tender.

8 Peel the small onions, and remove the outer layers and root ends. Rinse well.

12 Serve the rabbit stew with caramelized onions, and garnish with chopped chervil.

CHICKEN BREASTS STUFFED WITH MUSHROOMS

SERVES : 6

PREPARATION TIME : 35 Minutes
COOKING TIME : 40 Minutes

Chicken breasts are stuffed with ground chicken meat, egg and finely chopped mushrooms. They are cooked and served with pleurote mushrooms and a sauce of reduced chicken stock enriched with butter. If pleurote mushrooms are not available, substitute with another variety.

INGREDIENTS

- ☐ 1 cup button mushrooms
- ☐ Juice ½ lemon
- ☐ ½ cup butter
- ☐ 1 tbsp crème fraîche (or heavy cream)
- ☐ 7 chicken breasts
- ☐ 1 egg, beaten
- ☐ 3 tbsps chopped parsley
- ☐ 12oz pleurote mushrooms (or other wild variety)
- ☐ 1 clove garlic (central shoot removed)
- ☐ 1½ cups chicken stock
- ☐ Fresh herbs (chervil)
- ☐ Salt and pepper

1 Trim the stems of the button mushrooms. Wash lightly and set aside to drain.

2 Cut the mushrooms in four, then chop finely in a food processor with the lemon juice.

3 Melt 3½ tbsp of the butter in a frying pan. When bubbling, add the mushrooms, and sauté for 10 minutes over a high heat, stirring frequently.

4 Add the cream, salt and pepper to taste, and sauté for another 5 minutes. Allow to cool.

5

Process one skinned chicken breast until minced, then add ¹/₂ the beaten egg. Season well. Mix into the cooled mushroom with 1 tbsp chopped parsley.

6

Cut open the remaining breasts lengthwise, but do not cut through completely. Season.

7

Brush the insides of the opened chicken breasts with the remaining beaten egg. Fill each with some of the stuffing. Reconstruct and set aside.

8

Steam the stuffed breasts for 15 minutes.

9

Trim the stalks of the pleurote mushrooms, wash lightly, and drain thoroughly. Slice the mushrooms thinly.

10

Sauté the mushrooms in 2 tbsps of butter over medium heat. Add 1 tbsp parsley, the garlic, and salt and pepper. Cook for 10 minutes.

11

Reduce the stock by half, add 1 tbsp parsley, then gradually mix in 2 tbsps butter in small pieces using a hand-held electric blender.

12

Serve the stuffed chicken breasts with the pleurote mushrooms and the butter sauce. Garnish with fresh chervil.

GUINEA HEN
WITH CABBAGE
PANCAKES
AND PRUNES

SERVES : 4

PREPARATION TIME : 35 Minutes
COOKING TIME : 1 Hour 20 Minutes

*In this original and unusual recipe, a guinea
hen is steamed in a casserole with diced root
vegetables and prunes. The cooking liquid is
reduced to make a sauce. The dish is served
with a purée of cabbage, mixed with egg and
garlic and cooked like a crepe.*

GUINEA HEN WITH CABBAGE PANCAKES AND PRUNES

INGREDIENTS

- ☐ 2 carrots
- ☐ 1 onion
- ☐ Bouquet garni (parsley, thyme, bay leaf)
- ☐ 1 ready-to-cook guinea hen
- ☐ 5 tbsps olive oil
- ☐ 3 tbsps butter
- ☐ 12 prunes
- ☐ 1 cup chicken stock
- ☐ ½ white cabbage
- ☐ 4 cups milk
- ☐ 1 bunch chives
- ☐ 3 eggs
- ☐ ½ clove garlic, chopped (central shoot removed)
- ☐ Fresh herbs
- ☐ Salt and pepper

1   Dice the carrot finely. Chop the onion. Make a bouquet garni, by tying together the parsley, thyme and bay leaf.

2   Season the guinea hen and sear it on all sides in 2 tbsps of oil and half the butter, in a frying pan.

3   Remove the guinea hen. To the same pan add the carrot, onion and prunes, and sauté. Do not allow to color too much.

4   Put back the guinea hen, pour in the stock, add the bouquet garni, cover, and cook on a low heat for 30 minutes.

5 Open the cabbage, separate the leaves, cut out the stalks, then shred the leaves finely.

6 In a large saucepan, cook the cabbage in salted milk, covered, for 40 minutes on a moderate heat.

7 Strain after cooking, then blend smooth with ¼ cup of the cooking milk. Chop the chives.

8 Place the cabbage purée in a bowl, whisk in the eggs, chives, garlic, salt and pepper.

9 Heat the remaining oil and butter in a small frying pan. Use the cabbage mixture to make 4 pancakes.

10 Cook each one for 5 minutes on one side, turn, and cook for 4 minutes more over a low heat.

11 When the guinea hen is cooked through, remove, drain, and cut into 4. Remove the bouquet garni, and reserve the juice.

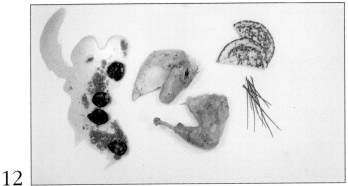

12 Serve the guinea hen portions with a little of the juice, the vegetables, and prunes and the cabbage pancakes, garnished with chopped herbs (chives).

MARINATED STEAK

WITH

CORIANDER

SERVES : 6

PREPARATION TIME : 40 Minutes
COOKING TIME : 1 Hour 10 Minutes
MARINADE : 2 Hours

A quickly prepared dish of steak marinated in white wine and coriander, a spice which gives a bitter-sweet flavor. The meat is quickly fried and served with individual carrot mousses and a sauce made from the marinade, enriched with cream.

INGREDIENTS

- ☐ 1 carrot
- ☐ ½ onion
- ☐ Bouquet garni (parsley, thyme, bay leaf)
- ☐ 6 (2lbs) tender beef steaks
- ☐ 40 coriander seeds
- ☐ 1 cup white wine
- ☐ 1lb carrots
- ☐ 2 tbsps crème fraîche (or sour cream)
- ☐ 4 eggs
- ☐ ½ tsp cinnamon
- ☐ 2 tbsps butter, melted
- ☐ ¾ cup heavy cream
- ☐ 2 tbsps oil
- ☐ Fresh herbs (chervil)
- ☐ Salt and pepper

1 Peel and dice the carrot and the onion. Make a bouquet garni by tying together the parsley, thyme and bay leaf.

2 Place the meat in a glass baking pan. Add 30 crushed coriander seeds, the onion, the carrot and the bouquet garni. Cover with the wine.

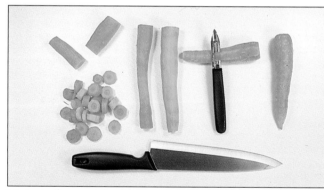

3 Marinate the meat for 2 hours. Peel the 1lb carrots and slice into rounds.

4 Boil the sliced carrots in salted water for approximately 20 minutes.

5 Strain the cooked carrots, reserving the water. Blend smooth in a food processor, adding a little cooking water, if necessary.

9 Remove the meat and bouquet garni from the marinade. In a saucepan, reduce the marinade by half over a high heat. Strain the reduced marinade through a fine sieve.

6 In a bowl, beat the crème fraîche into the carrot purée. Beat in the eggs and cinnamon. Season with salt and pepper.

10 Blend the cream into the marinade with a hand-held electric blender, adding the remaining coriander seeds. Return the vegetables to the sauce, and keep warm over hot water.

7 Brush 6 small molds with 1 tsp melted butter.

11 In a frying pan, melt the remaining butter with the oil. Dry the steaks with kitchen paper. Sear, season and cook to taste (2-10 minutes).

8 Fill the molds ¾ full with the carrot mixture. Cook in a "bain-marie" in a low oven 300°F for 30 to 40 minutes.

12 Serve the steaks sliced and spread into fan shapes, with the carrot mousses and marinade sauce. Garnish with chopped chervil.

MINUTE STEAK

AND

POTATOES AU GRATIN

SERVES : 6

PREPARATION TIME : 35 Minutes
COOKING TIME : 1 Hour 45 Minutes

An elegant meat and potato dish. Entrecôte steak is cooked quickly and served with a red wine sauce and a traditional "gratin dauphinois", sliced potato baked with butter and cream, and browned in the oven with cheese.

MINUTE STEAK AND POTATOES AU GRATIN

INGREDIENTS

☐ 2 shallots
☐ 2¼lbs potatoes
☐ 1 cup heavy cream
☐ 1 cup milk
☐ Nutmeg
☐ 2 tbsps butter, melted
☐ 1 clove garlic, chopped (central shoot removed)
☐ 1 tbsp chopped parsley
☐ ½ cup port
☐ ¼ cup red wine
☐ ¼ cup heavy cream
☐ 1lb 6oz sirloin steak
☐ 4 tbsps oil
☐ Fresh herbs (chervil)
☐ Salt and pepper

1 Peel and chop the shallots finely. Set aside for the sauce.

2 Peel the potatoes with a vegetable peeler. Immerse in cold water to prevent discoloration.

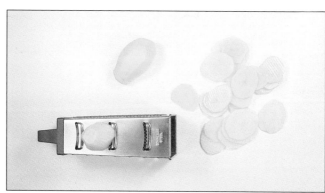

3 With the help of a vegetable slicer, slice the potatoes.

4 In a bowl, mix together the 1 cup cream, milk, salt, pepper and a pinch of nutmeg.

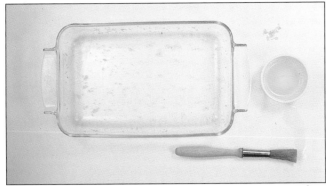

5 Brush a glass ovenproof pan with butter, and sprinkle with finely chopped garlic.

9 Mix in the ¼ cup cream with a hand-held electric blender, season to taste and keep warm over hot water.

6 Alternate layers of potato and parsley in the dish.

10 Cut the steak into very thin slices with a long, sharp knife.

7 Pour the cream and milk mixture over the potatoes. Cover with foil, and cook for about 1 hour 45 minutes in a moderate oven 350ºF.

11 Heat a little oil in a frying pan, and fry the steaks for approximately 30 seconds each side or longer, if prefered.

8 In a saucepan, reduce the port, shallots and red wine by ¾ (approximately 10 to 15 minutes).

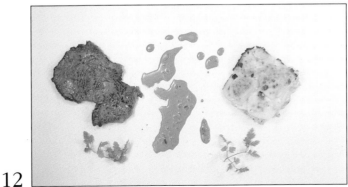

12 Serve the steaks immediately with a little sauce, accompanied with the potatoes au gratin. Garnish with the chervil.

BOILED BEEF
À LA PROVENÇALE

SERVES : 6

PREPARATION TIME : 50 Minutes
COOKING TIME : 3 Hours 15 Minutes

*Several different cuts of beef are simmered
slowly with root vegetables and herbs in an
old-style way. The dish is served with croutons,
garnished with bone marrow, a vinaigrette
sauce and a home-made garlic mayonnaise
called "aïoli".*

INGREDIENTS

☐ 3 carrots
☐ 6 small turnips
☐ ¼ cabbage
☐ 1 leek
☐ Bouquet garni (parsley, thyme, bay leaf)
☐ 1lb thick round steak
☐ 1lb chuck steak
☐ 1lb braising steak
☐ 2 marrow bones
☐ 1 onion, stuck with 2 whole cloves
☐ 5 peppercorns
☐ 1 egg yolk
☐ 1 cup olive oil
☐ 1 tsp mustard
☐ 2 cloves garlic (central shoot removed)
☐ 12 slices French bread
☐ 2 shallots, chopped
☐ 1 tbsp vinegar
☐ 2 tbsps oil
☐ Coarse salt
☐ Fresh herbs (chervil)
☐ Salt and pepper

1 Peel the carrots and turnips. Trim the cabbage, removing the hard core. Cut open and wash the leek. Wash the parsley.

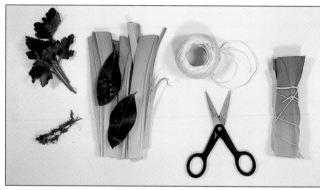

2 Make a large bouquet garni with the cut-open leek, parsley, thyme and bay leaf. Tie together securely with string and set aside.

3 Place the meat and bones in a large pan and cover with water. Bring to a boil and skim the foam off the top, as necessary.

4 Add the whole turnips, carrots, clove-studded onion, bouquet garni, peppercorns and salt. Remove the marrow bones after 10 minutes. Simmer the rest, covered, for 3 hours.

5 Shake the marrow from the bones. Allow to cool. For the mayonnaise, whisk together the egg yolks, mustard, salt and pepper.

9 When the meat is cooked, remove and cut into even slices.

6 Whisk in the oil, drop by drop. When thick, add the finely chopped garlic and mix well.

10 Remove the vegetables and cut into neat shapes.

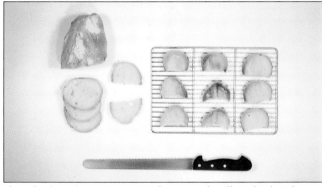

7 Slice the bread into attractive shapes and grill on both sides.

11 Cut up the cold marrow, place on the bread croutes, then sprinkle over a little coarse salt. Heat in a moderate oven just before serving.

8 Make a vinaigrette dressing by mixing together the shallots, salt, pepper, vinegar and olive oil. Set aside.

12 Serve the sliced meat with the vegetables, accompanied with the mayonnaise, vinaigrette dressing and marrow croutes. Sprinkle with fresh chervil.

STEAK WITH RED WINE SAUCE AND GREEN PEPPERCORNS

SERVES : 6

PREPARATION TIME : 45 Minutes
COOKING TIME : 45 Minutes

*This is an easy-to-prepare dish of fried steak
with a red wine and mushroom sauce spiced
with green peppercorns. It is served with sautéed
fresh artichoke hearts.*

INGREDIENTS

- [ ] 6 globe artichokes
- [ ] 1 lemon (juice and peel)
- [ ] ¾ cup mushrooms
- [ ] 2 shallots, chopped
- [ ] 4 sprigs parsley
- [ ] 10 green peppercorns
- [ ] 2 cups red wine
- [ ] 1 cup heavy cream
- [ ] 2lbs tender beef steak
- [ ] Mixed peppercorns, in a grinder
- [ ] 2 tbsps oil
- [ ] 4 tbsps butter
- [ ] Fresh herbs (chervil)
- [ ] Salt and pepper

1 Use medium-sized artichokes. Remove the artichoke stems.

2 Trim away all the leaves, without cutting too deeply into the artichoke heart. Cut away the choks, leaving the hearts.

3 Sprinkle the artichoke hearts with lemon juice to prevent discoloration. Add the lemon peel to a large quantity of water and boil the artichoke hearts for 20 minutes.

4 Trim the stalks off the mushrooms. Wash lightly and drain thoroughly. Slice finely.

5 Finely chop the shallots and parsley, which has been washed and well dried.

9 Cut the beef into 6 pieces, season with salt and freshly ground mixed peppercorns.

6 Place the shallots, green peppercorns, red wine and mushrooms in a saucepan. Bring to a boil and cook until reduced by ³/₄. Set aside.

10 In a frying pan, melt 3 tbsps of the butter with the oil, and cook the steaks to taste. Heat the remaining butter in a separate frying pan.

7 When the artichoke hearts are cooked, cool in cold water. Remove the remaining "bearded" center with a spoon, then cube.

11 Sauté the artichoke hearts, sprinkle over the parsley, and season to taste. Serve the steaks with the red wine sauce and the artichoke hearts.

8 Add the cream to the reduced sauce, mix well and reheat gently. Season to taste, then whisk well.

12 Garnish with a few freshly chopped herbs.

BRAISED BEEF

WITH

CARAMELIZED

CARROTS

SERVES : 6

PREPARATION TIME : 30 Minutes
COOKING TIME : 2 Hours 30 Minutes

A relatively economical main course, braising beef is slowly cooked with bacon, small onions and aromatic herbs and served with lightly caramelized sautéed carrots to add a slightly sweet taste.

BRAISED BEEF WITH CARAMELIZED CARROTS

INGREDIENTS

- ☐ 2½lbs braising steak
- ☐ 1 onion
- ☐ ½ stick celery
- ☐ 2lbs carrots
- ☐ 1 cup small onions
- ☐ 6oz smoked bacon (in one piece)
- ☐ 3 tbsps olive oil
- ☐ 2 cups red wine
- ☐ 3 cloves garlic (central shoot removed)
- ☐ Bouquet garni (parsley, thyme, bay leaf)
- ☐ 5 tsps sugar
- ☐ Fresh herbs (chervil)
- ☐ Salt and pepper

1 Cut the meat into thick slices, then into large, even-sized cubes.

2 Chop the onion and the celery finely.

3 Peel the carrots, cut them into chunks, slice in two lengthwise, then trim into long, oval shapes. (Keep the trimmings.)

4 Soak the small onions for 1 minute in warm water, and peel with a small, sharp knife (soaking facilitates peeling.).

5 Cut off the bacon rind and cut the bacon first into slices and then into small pieces.

9 Cook the carrots in boiling salted water for 8 minutes. Drain and rinse.

6 Heat the oil and sear the meat on each side, browning lightly (approximately 2 minutes).

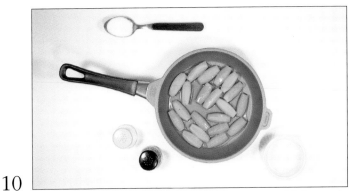

10 Glaze the carrots in a frying pan with the sugar and 5 tbsps of water on a gentle heat, shaking the pan continuously until the liquid has evaporated.

7 Add the celery, onion and carrot trimmings to the meat. Fry for 1 minute.

11 Remove the meat with a fork, place in another casserole, strain the stock over the beef and add the onions and the bacon. Cook for 20 minutes more.

8 Pour over the wine, add the garlic, bouquet garni, salt and pepper, and 2 cups water. Cover and simmer for 2 hours 30 minutes.

12 Serve the braised beef, onions and glazed carrots garnished with fresh, chopped herbs.

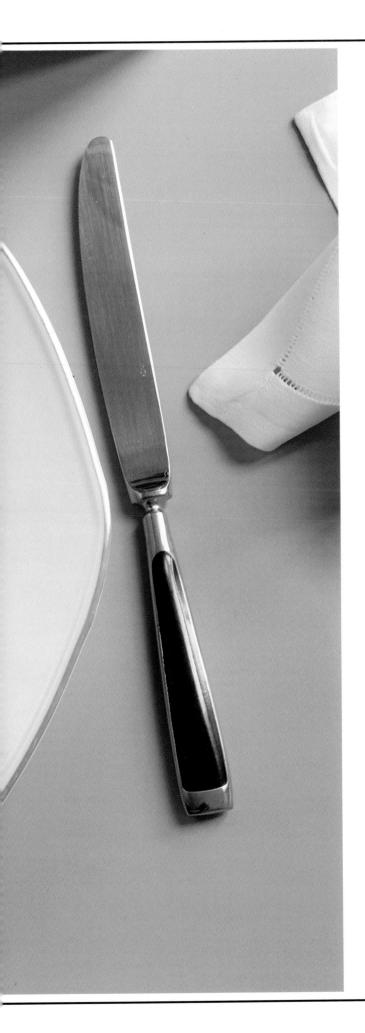

PORK FILLET

WITH

MUSTARD SAUCE

SERVES : 6

PREPARATION TIME : 35 Minutes
COOKING TIME : 1 Hour 10 Minutes

*A classic combination. Roast fillet of pork is
stuffed with garlic and prunes and served with
a grain mustard sauce accompanied with
shredded white cabbage sautéed with bacon.*

INGREDIENTS

☐ 1 large pork fillet
☐ 8 prunes
☐ 1 tsp chopped garlic, (central shoot removed)
☐ 4 tbsps olive oil
☐ 2 spring cabbages
☐ 8oz bacon
☐ 2 tbsps butter
☐ ¼ cup white wine
☐ ½ cup chicken stock
☐ ¾ cup heavy cream
☐ 2 tbsps mustard
☐ Fresh herbs (chervil)
☐ Salt and pepper

1 Cut open the pork fillet lengthwise, but do not cut all the way through. Pit the prunes.

2 Season the meat all over, spread the prunes and the garlic down the center of the fillet.

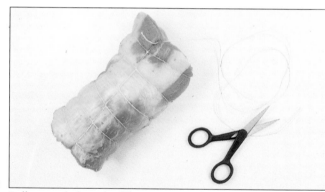

3 Roll up and close the fillet. Secure well with kitchen string.

4 In 4 tbsps of oil, sear and brown the meat on all sides, then transfer to a hot oven 400°F for 40 minutes.

5 Remove the outer cabbage leaves and discard. Separate the leaves, wash and slice finely.

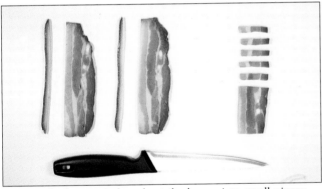

6 Blanch for 3 minutes in boiling, salted water, then plunge in cold water. Set aside to drain.

7 Remove the bacon rind, and cut the bacon into small pieces.

8 In the butter, fry the bacon quickly to brown it lightly.

9 Add the well-drained cabbage to the bacon. Season, mix well, and cook gently for 20 minutes, stirring occasionally.

10 When cooked, remove the pork from the oven, pour off any excess fat, and deglaze with the wine. Stir and pour into a saucepan ; reduce the sauce for 5 minutes. Add the cream.

11 Add the mustard, and blend with a hand-held electric blender. Heat through, but do not boil. Slice the meat.

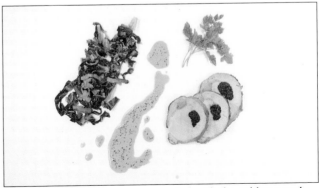

12 Serve the pork in slices, accompanied with the cabbage and sauce. Garnish with fresh, chopped chervil.

CARAMELIZED PORK SPARERIBS

WITH

LEMON GRASS

SERVES : 6

PREPARATION TIME : 1 Hour 30 Minutes
COOKING TIME : 40 Minutes

This is an Oriental-inspired dish of pork spareribs baked in the oven with soy sauce, honey and lemon grass until lightly caramelized. The sweet and savory taste is emphasized with a side dish of puréed sweet potatoes.

INGREDIENTS

- ☐ 2½lbs pork spareribs
- ☐ 1 carrot
- ☐ 1 onion
- ☐ 1 bouquet garni (parsley, thyme, bay leaf)
- ☐ 1 stalk lemon grass
- ☐ 2 tbsps honey
- ☐ 1 tbsp wine vinegar
- ☐ 3 tbsps soy sauce
- ☐ 1 clove garlic (central shoot removed)
- ☐ 5 slices ginger root, peeled and chopped
- ☐ 2lbs sweet potatoes
- ☐ 1 tbsp olive oil
- ☐ 1 onion, chopped
- ☐ 2 tbsps heavy cream
- ☐ ½ cup milk
- ☐ Fresh herbs (chives)
- ☐ Salt and pepper

1 Separate the spareribs, cutting between the bones. Cut the bone in half lengthwise, if too long.

2 Peel and slice the onion and carrot.

3 In a flameproof casserole, cover the spareribs, onion, carrot and bouquet garni with water. Bring to a boil.

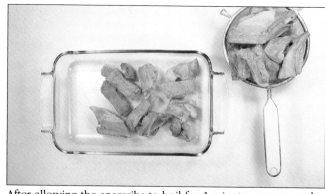

4 After allowing the spareribs to boil for 1 minute, remove and drain together with the onion, carrot and bouquet garni. Place the ribs in a glass baking pan.

5 Slice the lemon grass thinly lengthwise. Then chop finely.

6 In a bowl, whip together the honey, vinegar, soy sauce, lemon grass, garlic and the ginger. Stir in 1 tbsp water.

7 Pour this mixture over the spareribs, mix together well, and cook for approximately 40 minutes in a hot oven 400°F.

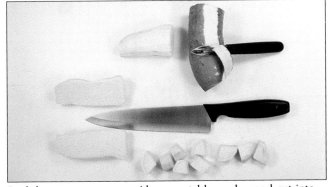

8 Peel the sweet potatoes with a vegetable peeler, and cut into small, even-sized pieces.

9 Simmer the sweet potatoes for 35 minutes in a large quantity of salted water with the chopped onion and 1 tbsp olive oil.

10 As the ribs are baking, remove them frequently from the oven and stir them with a wooden spatula.

11 Drain the sweet potatoes when cooked, and mash to a purée. Stir in the milk and cream. Season to taste, and keep warm over hot water.

12 Remove the caramelized spare ribs from the oven, and arrange over a bed of sweet potato purée. Garnish with the chives.

LAMB STEW À LA PROVENÇALE

SERVES : 6

PREPARATION TIME : 1 Hour 30 Minutes
COOKING TIME : 1 Hour 30 Minutes

*Boneless lamb shoulder meat is slowly stewed
with garlic and basil for full flavor. The
Mediterranean-style vegetable accompaniment
is a gratin of eggplant and tomato which goes
wonderfully with the lamb.*

LAMB STEW À LA PROVENÇALE

INGREDIENTS

- ☐ 4½lbs lamb shoulder
- ☐ 30 leaves fresh basil
- ☐ 3 cloves garlic (central shoot removed)
- ☐ 1 onion
- ☐ 3 tbsps olive oil
- ☐ ½ cup white wine
- ☐ Bouquet garni (parsley, thyme, bay leaf)
- ☐ 1 large eggplant
- ☐ 3 tomatoes
- ☐ Flour for coating
- ☐ 1 cup olive oil
- ☐ 1 cup shredded cheese (Cheddar or Gruyère)
- ☐ Extra chopped fresh basil
- ☐ Salt and pepper

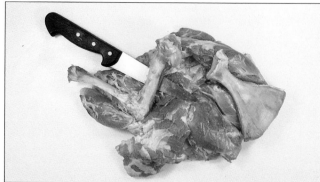

1 Using a sharp knife, cut all around the lamb shoulder bone to remove from the meat.

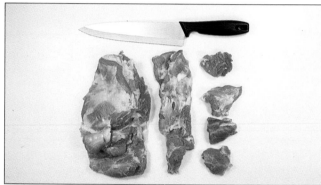

2 Trim away any substantial amounts of fat. Cut the meat into even-sized cubes.

3 Remove the leaves of basil from the stalks. Reserve these and chop the leaves finely. Chop the garlic finely. Chop the onion finely.

4 Heat 3 tbsps oil in a frying pan, and sear the meat on all sides over a high heat until the meat is lightly browned.

5 Pour off the excess fat, and add the chopped onion, garlic and basil leaves. Sauté for 1 minute.

6 Deglaze the pan with the white wine. Reduce until almost evaporated, add 1 cup water and the bouquet garni. Season. Add the basil stalks and cook, covered, for 1 hour.

7 Slice the eggplant and tomato into rounds.

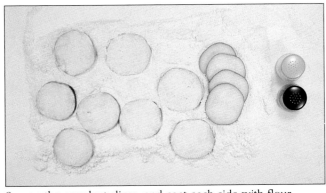

8 Season the eggplant slices, and coat each side with flour.

9 Sauté the eggplant slices a few at a time in the remaining oil. Drain on paper towels.

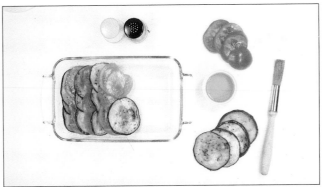

10 Interlace the eggplant and tomato slices in the bottom of an ovenproof pan. Season again.

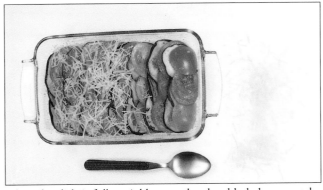

11 When the dish is full, sprinkle over the shredded cheese, and bake for 25 minutes in a hot oven 400°F.

12 Serve the lamb stew with the eggplant and tomato gratin. Garnish with extra chopped basil.

LAMB NOISETTES

WITH

CAULIFLOWER

SERVES : 6

PREPARATION TIME : 1 Hour
COOKING TIME : 1 Hour 10 Minutes

*A gastronomic preparation of saddle of lamb
that is rolled with ham and seared before
baking. It is served with a sauce of puréed
cauliflower and a delicate side dish of braised
lettuce.*

INGREDIENTS

- ☐ 1 saddle of lamb (approximately 4½lbs)
- ☐ 9 very thin slices Parma ham
- ☐ ¼ cauliflower
- ☐ 2 cups milk
- ☐ 3 lettuces
- ☐ 5 tbsps butter, melted
- ☐ ¼ heavy cream
- ☐ Nutmeg
- ☐ 3 tbsps oil
- ☐ 10 black olives
- ☐ Fresh herbs (chervil)
- ☐ Salt and pepper

1 Bone the saddle of lamb, and cut off any excess fat and gristle. Cut the meat into small medallions.

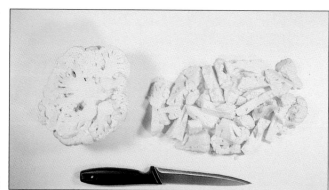

2 Cut the Parma ham into strips, lengthwise. Roll around each medallion and secure neatly with kitchen string.

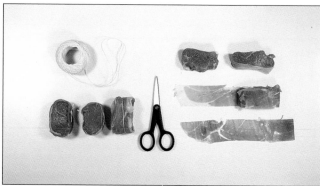

3 Break the cauliflower into small pieces, discarding any hard stalks.

4 Cook the cauliflower in the milk, seasoned with salt and pepper, for 30 minutes.

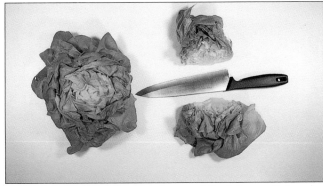

5 Remove and discard the outer leaves of the lettuces. Cut each one in two.

6 Plunge the two halves of lettuce into boiling salted water for 3 minutes. Repeat with all the lettuce halves (drain the lettuce and refresh in cold water).

7 Squeeze the excess water from the lettuces. Shape and place them in a buttered, ovenproof pan and bake for 30 minutes in a hot oven 400ºF with 4 tbsps water.

8 Blend the cauliflower, cooking milk and cream in a food processor until smooth. Pour into a pan and season with salt, pepper and nutmeg.

9 Heat the oil and the remaining butter in a pan and sear the lamb medallions on each side. Transfer to a hot oven 400ºF and cook for 8 to 15 minutes.

10 Pit the olives and chop them finely.

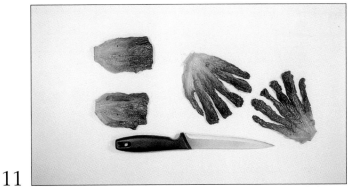

11 Remove the cooked lettuces from the oven and cut and shape into fans using a sharp knife.

12 Cut off the string from the meat. Serve decoratively with the lettuces. Accompany with the reheated cauliflower sauce, garnished with the chopped olives and fresh chervil.

VEAL BLANQUETTE

WITH

ROQUEFORT

SERVES : 6

PREPARATION TIME : 25 Minutes
COOKING TIME : 2 Hours

This classic French veal stew in a creamy white sauce is modernized with the addition of blue cheese. The pungently flavored blanquette is served with a simple rice pilaf.

INGREDIENTS

☐ 2lbs veal shoulder
☐ 1 leek
☐ 2 carrots
☐ Bouquet garni (parsley, thyme bay leaf)
☐ 8oz mushrooms
☐ 1 onion, chopped
☐ 6 tbsps butter
☐ 1¼ cup rice
☐ 1 tbsp flour
☐ 6oz Roquefort, crumbled
☐ ¾ cup heavy cream
☐ ½ bunch chives, chopped
☐ 1 tbsp chopped parsley
☐ Salt and pepper

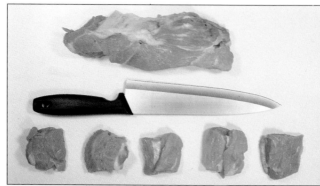

1 Cut the meat into even-sized pieces, without removing the excess fat (the fat enhances the flavor of the dish).

2 In a flameproof casserole, cover the meat with water, bring to a boil, cook for 4 minutes, skimming the surface of the water from time to time. Remove the meat and discard the water.

3 Wash, peel and chop the leek and carrots finely.

4 In a flameproof casserole, melt 2 tbsps of the butter, sauté the leek, carrot and bouquet garni. Add the meat and cover with water. Season with salt and simmer, covered, for 1¼ hours.

5 Strain the mixture through a fine sieve, reserving the meat and stock.

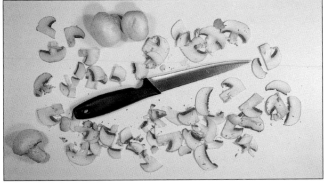

6 Remove the stalks of the mushrooms, wash and chop the caps finely.

7 In an ovenproof casserole, sauté the chopped onion and mushrooms in 2 tbsps butter for 2 minutes. Preheat the oven 425°F.

8 Add the rice and cook, stirring constantly, over a low heat for 2 minutes. Add 2 cups of the cooking stock. Season. Cook, covered, in the preheated oven, for 20 minutes.

9 In a saucepan, melt 2 tbsps butter, stir in the flour and cook for 1 minute over a low heat. Add 1 cup of the cooking stock, stir and allow to thicken for 2 minutes.

10 Add the Roquefort and the cream. Blend with a hand-held electric blender. Season if necessary.

11 Add the meat to the sauce and reheat over a low heat for approximately 5 minutes.

12 Serve the veal blanquette with the rice, garnished with the chopped chives and parsley.

VEAL KIDNEYS

WITH

CREAMED SPINACH

SERVES : 6

PREPARATION TIME : 20 Minutes
COOKING TIME : 35 Minutes

Veal kidneys retain their tenderness when baked "en papillote" or in little foil packages. The dish is served with creamed, puréed spinach and accompanied by crisp, deep-fried straw potatoes.

INGREDIENTS

☐ 3 veal kidneys
☐ 3 tsps Cognac
☐ 1lb spinach
☐ 1lb good quality potatoes
☐ Oil for deep-frying
☐ 1½ cups heavy cream
☐ Fresh herbs (chervil)
☐ Salt and pepper

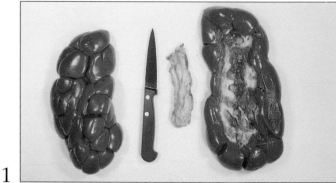

1 Devein and cut out any fat from the kidneys. Using the tip of a sharp, small knife remove all the white parts.

2 Arrange the 3 kidneys on 3 sheets of foil, season with salt and pepper, and sprinkle with the Cognac.

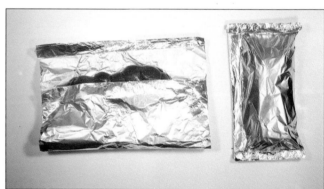

3 Fold up the foil to form sealed packages. Set aside until ready to cook.

4 Trim the stalks from the spinach, and wash thoroughly.

5 Plunge the spinach in boiling, salted water, and cook for 5 minutes.

9 When lightly browned, drain the potatoes on paper towels. Cook the kidneys in a hot oven 400°F for 8 to 15 minutes.

6 Drain and rinse the spinach; squeeze out the excess water. Chop as finely as possible.

10 Place the chopped spinach and the cream in a flameproof casserole. Heat through gently, season, and blend with a hand-held electric blender.

7 Peel the potatoes and cut into matchsticks. Rinse well, then dry on a kitchen towel.

11 Remove the kidneys from the oven, but allow them to rest in the foil for 5 minutes. Remove and slice.

8 In a large, deep frying pan, preheat the oil and fry the potatoes in several batches.

12 Serve the sliced kidneys arranged in rounds, surrounded by the creamed spinach, with the straw potatoes in the center. Sprinkle with fresh chervil.

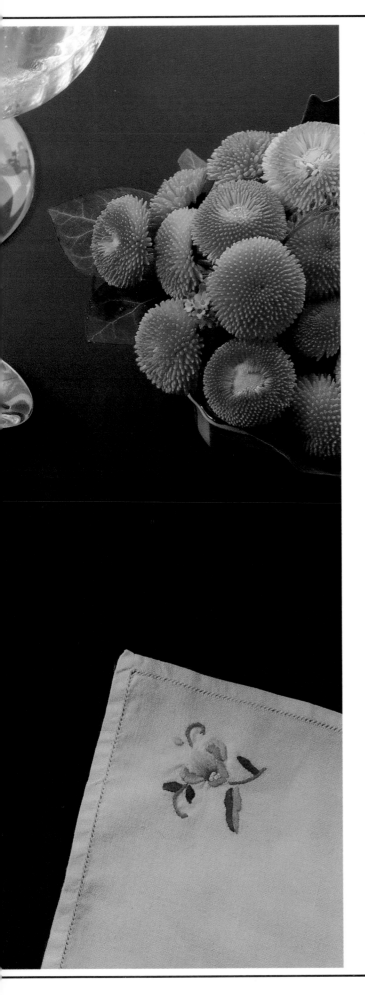

EXOTIC FRUIT SOUP

WITH

COCONUT

SERVES : 6

PREPARATION TIME : 40 Minutes

*A refreshing dessert, the fruits can be varied
according to season and availability. Serve in
soup bowls with vanilla or coconut ice cream
and all the natural juices from the fruit.*

INGREDIENTS

- ☐ 1 mango
- ☐ 1 papaya
- ☐ 1 banana
- ☐ 1 kiwi fruit
- ☐ 1 small pineapple
- ☐ 12 rambutans or litchis
- ☐ 2 oranges
- ☐ 2 grapefruit
- ☐ 1 tbsp coconut liqueur
- ☐ Sugar (optional)
- ☐ 2 cups coconut ice cream
- ☐ 1 tbsp grated coconut
- ☐ Mint leaves

1 Peel the mango with a small sharp knife, taking care not to remove too much of the flesh.

2 Cut the mango into slices, right down to the stone.

3 Cut the papaya in half, peel and remove the pips from the center.

4 Cut the papaya halves into thin, crosswise slices.

5 Peel the banana and kiwi fruit and slice into rounds.

6 With a sharp knife, cut the peel off the pineapple.

7 Cut out the pineapple "eyes" with the tip of a vegetable peeler. Cut the flesh into even-sized chunks.

8 Peel the rambutans or litchis, pull open the fruit and remove the stones. If this is too difficult, leave the stones in place.

9 Squeeze the juice from the oranges and the grapefruit. Add the coconut liqueur.

10 Mix together all the fruit with the juices and liqueur, and sweeten if necessary. Chill in the refrigerator.

11 Just before serving, scoop out balls of ice cream and roll them in the grated coconut.

12 Serve the fruit soup immediately, garnished with chopped or snipped mint.

PEAR AND HONEY CRUMBLE

SERVES : 6

PREPARATION TIME : 30 Minutes
COOKING TIME : 35 Minutes

*A French chef's version of a classic crumble,
pears are sautéed in honey and butter with the
addition of raisins and sautéed rhubarb. The
fruits are layered and topped with a delicate
crumble and baked in the oven.*

INGREDIENTS

- ☐ 6 pears (or apples)
- ☐ 3 tbsps butter
- ☐ ¼ cup currants
- ☐ 3 tbsps liquid honey
- ☐ 2 cups all-purpose flour
- ☐ ½ cup butter
- ☐ ¼ cup ground almonds
- ☐ ¼ cup sugar
- ☐ 4 large sticks rhubarb
- ☐ 2 tbsps butter
- ☐ 2 tbsps sugar
- ☐ ½ cup heavy cream
- ☐ 1 tbsp unsweetened cocoa

1 Peel the pears with a vegetable peeler. Remove the core with a melon baller.

2 Halve the pears lengthwise and then cube.

3 Heat 3 tbsps butter until hot and sauté the pear cubes.

4 When golden brown, add the currants and honey, mix well and remove from the heat.

5 Turn the pear mixture into a glass baking pan and allow to cool.

6 To make the crumble, rub the ½ cup butter into the flour with the ground almonds.

7 Work in the ¼ cup sugar, to obtain a coarse, crumbly mixture.

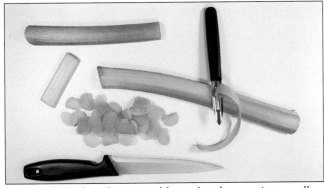

8 Peel the rhubarb with a vegetable peeler, then cut into small chunks.

9 Sauté the rhubarb in the remaining 2 tbsps butter, add remaining sugar and cook for 3 minutes more.

10 Spread the cooled rhubarb mixture over the pear mixture.

11 Sprinkle the crumble topping over to cover the fruit completely. Cook in a hot oven 400°F for 25 minutes.

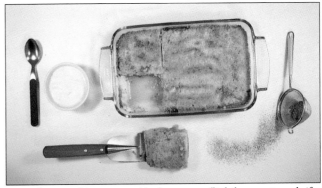

12 Serve the crumble warm with the cream (lightly sweetened, if desired), sprinkled with cocoa powder.

CHOCOLATE GANACHE

SERVES : 6

PREPARATION TIME : 1 Hour
COOKING TIME : 5 Minutes
CHILLING TIME : 6 Hours

A rich chocolate terrine consisting of layers of ladyfingers, a dark chocolate mousse and raspberry jam. The ganache is garnished with fresh orange slices to add a little tartness.

INGREDIENTS

- ☐ 12oz semi-sweet chocolate
- ☐ ½ cup heavy cream
- ☐ 2 tbsps butter
- ☐ ¼ cup egg whites
- ☐ Pinch salt
- ☐ 1 package powdered gelatin
- ☐ 5 tbsps honey
- ☐ 20 ladyfingers
- ☐ 2 tbsps raspberry liqueur
- ☐ 2 tbsps water
- ☐ ½ cup raspberry jam
- ☐ 2 oranges

1 Cut the chocolate into fine shreds with a long, heavy knife.

2 Place the chocolate in a bowl, pour over the cream, heated to boiling point, and whip well.

3 Add the slightly softened butter to the above and whip well.

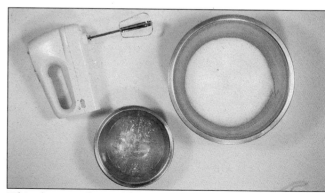

4 Whip the egg whites with a pinch of salt until stiff but not dry. Soak the gelatin in a little water. Bring the honey to a boil.

5 Remove the honey from the heat and stir in the softened gelatin. Gradually pour this over the egg whites, whipping continuously to form a meringue.

6 Fold the meringue carefully into the chocolate ganache, using a spatula.

7 Cut wax paper to fit a loaf pan, overhanging the sides. Place a layer of ladyfingers in the base. Pour over half of the ganache.

8 Mix the liqueur with 2 tbsps water and brush this over the remaining ladyfingers. Layer these over the ganache.

9 Spoon the jam over the ladyfingers. The jam should not be thick, but heat if necessary.

10 Pour over the remaining ganache. Pull the overhanging paper to cover the top neatly and freeze for 6 hours.

11 Peel the oranges down to the flesh. Cut into segments to serve with the chilled chocolate ganache.

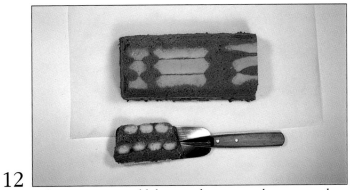

12 Before serving, unmold the ganache, remove the paper and cut into slices. Dip the knife into boiling water before cutting each slice.

SWEET
SABLÉ COOKIES
WITH
FRUIT

SERVES : 6

PREPARATION TIME : 40 Minutes
COOKING TIME : 25 Minutes

*Sablés, meaning sandy, are buttery shortcakes.
They are served with pastry cream, fresh fruit
and a custard sauce. Be creative in the last-
minute assembling and preparation of this
multi-ingredient dessert.*

INGREDIENTS

- [ ] 3 cups all-purpose flour, sifted
- [ ] ½ heaping cup sugar
- [ ] Pinch salt
- [ ] 1 egg
- [ ] ¾ cup butter
- [ ] 5 egg yolks
- [ ] ⅔ cup sugar
- [ ] 1 vanilla pod
- [ ] 2 cups milk
- [ ] 2 oranges
- [ ] 2 kiwi fruit
- [ ] 1 banana
- [ ] 30 raspberries
- [ ] 1 cup heavy cream
- [ ] 2 tbsps sugar
- [ ] 4 tsps unsweetened cocoa
- [ ] Fresh mint

1 Make the dough by mixing together the flour, ½ cup sugar, salt and egg. Work in with your fingers to obtain a fine, crumbly mixture.

2 Add the butter, cut into small pieces. Work in to make a firm dough. Form into a ball, flour lightly and chill.

3 Make a soft custard by mixing together the egg yolks and ½ cup sugar. Cut the vanilla bean in half, extract the seeds and add the seeds to the above.

4 Bring the milk to a boil and add it slowly to the egg and sugar. Pour back into the pan and place over a gentle heat.

5 Cook, stirring constantly, for 7 to 10 minutes, until thickened. Cool and then chill.

9 Place on a nonstick cookie sheet and cook in a hot oven 400ºF for 10 to 15 minutes. Allow to cool on the cookie sheet.

6 Prepare the fruit. Separate the oranges into segments, cut the kiwi fruit and banana into rounds. Leave the raspberries whole.

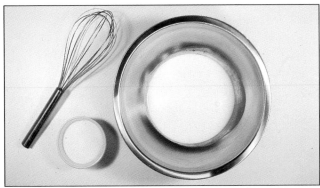

10 Place the cream in a bowl, freeze for 5 minutes then whip until slightly thickened.

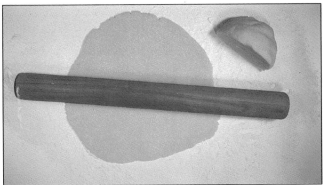

7 Remove the dough from the refrigerator 10 minutes before rolling. Roll out thinly with a floured rolling pin on a floured surface.

11 As the cream begins to thicken add the sugar and continue whipping until thick.

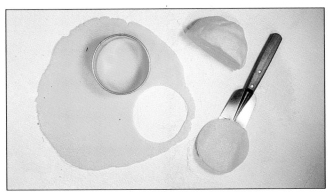

8 Cut out 12 medium-sized rounds with a biscuit cutter.

12 Assemble all the ingredients ; the cookie bases, custard, fruit and whipped cream. Arrange together as you like, and decorate with the sifted unsweetened cocoa.

ORANGE MERINGUE TART

SERVES : 6

PREPARATION TIME : 35 Minutes
COOKING TIME : 40 Minutes

*Here is a variation on the classic lemon
meringue pie. Fresh orange juice and orange
peel are essential for flavoring the filling.
The tart is topped with meringue, and
caramelized in the oven. Serve with
fresh soft fruits, if in season.*

INGREDIENTS

- ☐ 1 cup all-purpose flour
- ☐ 2 tbsps sugar
- ☐ 3 tbsps water
- ☐ 1 egg yolk
- ☐ ½ cup butter
- ☐ 2 oranges
- ☐ 6 eggs
- ☐ ¾ cup sugar
- ☐ ⅔ butter
- ☐ ½ cup dried beans
- ☐ 3 egg whites
- ☐ 3 tbsps confectioners' sugar
- ☐ Pinch salt

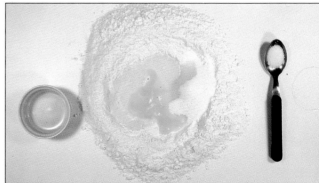

1 Make the dough. Pile the flour on your work surface or in a bowl. Make a well in the center and place the 2 tbsps sugar, salt, water and egg yolk in it.

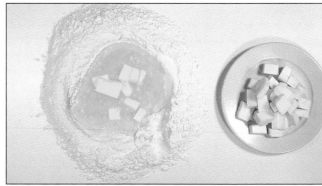

2 Work in the ingredients with your fingers to mix well. Add the ½ cup butter at room temperature, cut into small pieces.

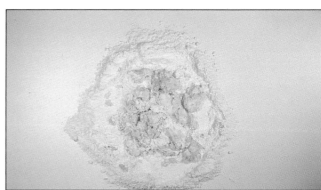

3 Mix in the butter to form a ball of dough. Sprinkle with flour and allow to rest in the refrigerator.

4 Cut off the zest of ½ orange with a vegetable peeler. Squeeze the juice from the 2 oranges.

5 Cut the zest into thin strips. Place in a saucepan of water, bring to a boil, strain and rinse. Set aside to drain.

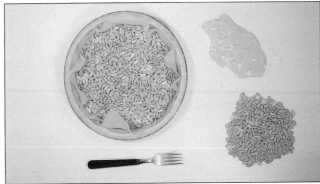

9 Roll the pastry to fit into a pie pan. Prick with a fork. Cover with wax paper, top with the beans and cook in the preheated oven for 25 minutes. Remove paper and beans and cool.

6 In a saucepan, whip together the orange juice, eggs, sugar, 2/3 cup butter and orange zest.

10 Whip the egg whites together with a pinch of salt and 1/2 the icing sugar. After 1 minute add the remaining sugar, whip until stiff.

7 Whip continuously over a gentle heat for about 10 minutes. The mixture will gradually thicken.

11 Spread the warm orange filling over the cooked, cooled pastry case. Pipe the meringue decoratively over the filling.

8 Take out the dough 10 minutes before rolling. Roll out on a floured surface. Preheat the oven 400°F.

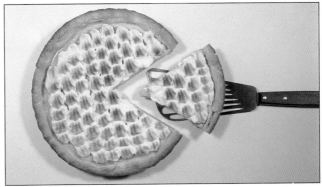

12 Brown the meringue lightly under a hot broiler. Serve when cool.

SPICE CAKE

SERVES : 6

PREPARATION TIME : 30 Minutes
COOKING TIME : 50 Minutes

*This sweet spice cake is based on a traditional
"quatre-quarts" cake which is the French
equivalent of our well-known Pound Cake. It is
served with a cinnamon custard sauce.*

INGREDIENTS

- ☐ ⅔ cup butter at room temperature
- ☐ 6 tbsps sugar
- ☐ 2 eggs
- ☐ 6oz flour
- ☐ 1 tsp baking powder
- ☐ ½ tsp ground ginger
- ☐ 1 tsp mixed spice powder
- ☐ 6 egg yolks
- ☐ 6 tbsps sugar
- ☐ 2 cups milk
- ☐ ½ tsp cinnamon
- ☐ 6 tbsps flaked almonds
- ☐ Small bunch fresh mint

1 In a bowl, beat ⅔ cup butter until soft.

2 Add the sugar, beating the mixture well for 3 minutes.

3 In another bowl, beat the eggs. Whip them gradually into the butter and sugar mixture.

4 Mix the baking powder, ginger and mixed spice into the flour. Add to the above and mix together well.

5 Grease a non-stick cake pan with the remaining butter, then pour in the cake mixture.

9 Cook over a very low heat, stirring constantly, until thickened (6 to 8 minutes). Remove from the heat.

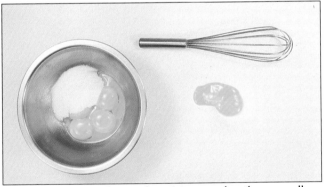

6 Cook the cake in a bain-marie in a moderate oven 350°F covered with a sheet of wax paper, for 40 minutes.

10 Toast the flaked almonds under a hot broilet, stirring as necessary until golden brown.

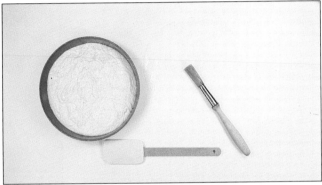

7 Make the egg custard sauce by mixing together the egg yolks and sugar. Bring the milk to a boil.

11 When the cake is done, (when an inserted blade comes out clean) turn out onto a cake rack to cool.

8 Add the cinnamon to the egg yolk mixture, then pour over the milk. Whip continuously, and pour back into the saucepan.

12 Cut into wedges, and serve with the cinnamon custard sauce, garnished with the flaked almonds and a few mint leaves.

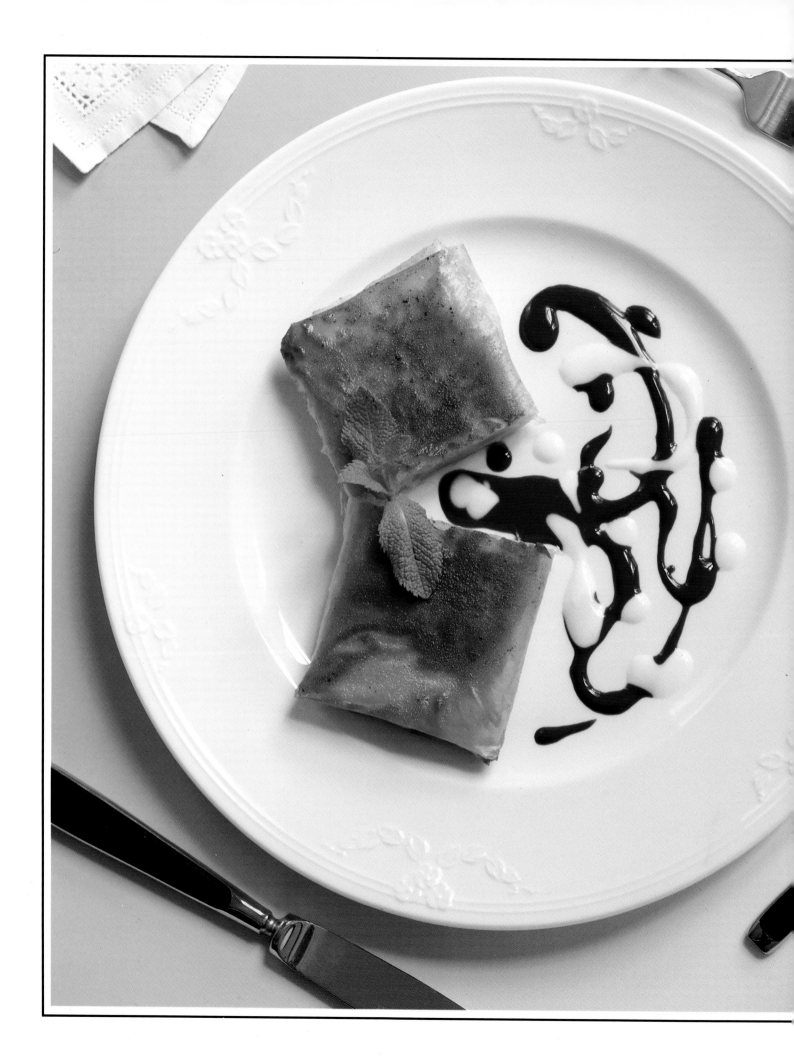

CRISP BANANA PASTRIES

WITH

CHOCOLATE SAUCE

SERVES : 6

PREPARATION TIME : 25 Minutes
COOKING TIME : 15 Minutes

*An original dessert sure to make an
impression. Little packages of filo dough are
filled with pastry cream, sliced bananas and
banana essence. They are first browned in
butter then baked and served with
a rich chocolate sauce.*

INGREDIENTS

- ☐ 2 egg yolks
- ☐ ¼ cup sugar
- ☐ 2 tbsps flour
- ☐ 1 cup pint milk
- ☐ ½ tsp banana essence
- ☐ 4 bananas
- ☐ 6 sheets filo dough
- ☐ 8oz chocolate
- ☐ 5 tbsps heavy cream
- ☐ 4 tsps sugar
- ☐ ½ cup milk
- ☐ 3 tbsps butter
- ☐ Few mint leaves
- ☐ 2 tbsps heavy cream

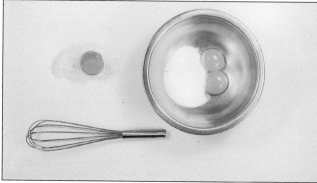

1 Make the pastry cream. In a bowl, mix together the egg yolks, sugar and the flour, until you obtain a thick, but smooth batter.

2 Bring the ¼ litre/½ pint milk to the boil and pour it over the egg yolk mixture, stirring rapidly. Pour this back into the saucepan.

3 Cook over a moderate heat, stirring constantly, until the mixture thickens as it comes to a boil. Stir in the banana essence, and allow to cool.

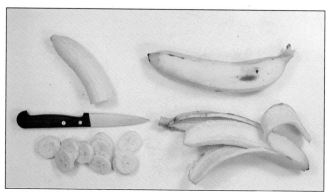

4 Peel the bananas and slice.

5 Spread 1 level tablespoon of sauce over the center of each sheet of filo dough.

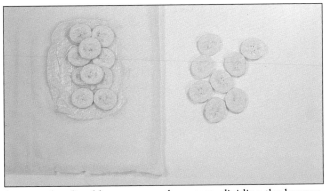

6 Arrange the sliced banana over the cream, dividing the banana evenly between the six sheets.

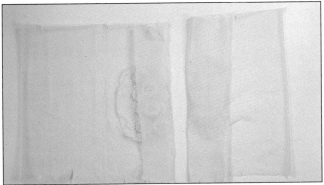

7 Fold the filo sheets into pastries by bringing one side up and over the filling.

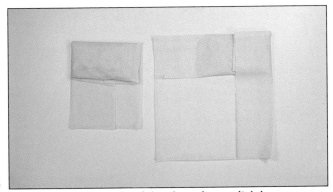

8 Fold over the other side of dough, and press lightly.

9 Chop the chocolate, and place in a bowl with the cream, the sugar and the milk. Melt over boiling water.

10 Once the chocolate has melted, mix it gently with a whisk. Keep warm. Preheat the oven 400ºF.

11 In a large frying pan, melt the butter and fry the pastries for approximately 2 minutes each side. Transfer to a non-stick baking pan and bake in the preheated oven for 5 minutes.

12 Serve with the hot chocolate sauce and a little heavy cream, if desired.

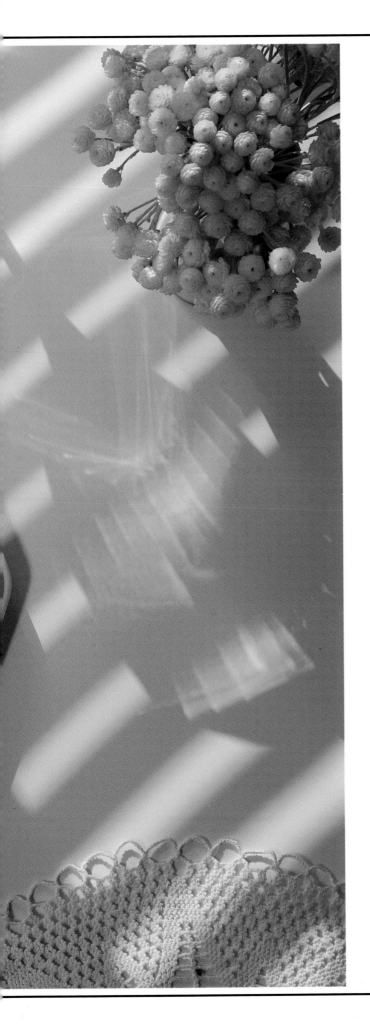

FROZEN KIWI MOUSSE

WITH

FRUIT PURÉE

SERVES : 6

PREPARATION TIME : 30 Minutes
COOKING TIME : 10 Minutes
SETTING TIME : 6 Hours

A very attractive and colorful dessert, which uses several different fruits. Individual mousses of puréed kiwi and cream are set in the freezer. They are served with a coulis of red fruit, either strawberry or raspberry, and a lemon-flavored banana purée.

INGREDIENTS

- ☐ 5 kiwis fruit
- ☐ 1½ packages powdered gelatin
- ☐ 1¾ cups cane sugar syrup
- ☐ 1½ cups heavy cream
- ☐ 8oz strawberries
- ☐ 2 bananas
- ☐ ½ lemon
- ☐ Fresh mint

1 Peel the kiwi fruit, cut each into 4 lengthwise and remove the woody core.

2 Soak the gelatin in water. Press the kiwi fruit through a sieve, adding 1 tbsp water, or purée in a food processor.

3 In a saucepan, heat 6 fl oz of the sugar syrup, and add the softened gelatin to the pan. Allow to cool and stir into the kiwi pulp. Mix well.

4 Place 6 fl oz of the cream in a bowl. Freeze for 5 minutes, then begin to whip.

5

Whip the cream gradually until thick and doubled in volume.

6

Using a spatula, fold the cream into the cooled kiwi mixture.

7

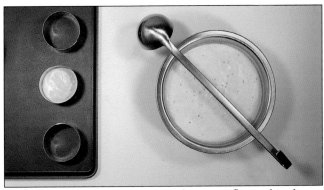

Place 6 stainless steel rings or ramekins on a flat cookie sheet and ladle the mousse into them. Set in the freezer.

8

Bring 6 fl oz of the sugar syrup to a boil and add the trimmed and washed strawberries. Remove from the heat and set aside for 5 minutes.

9

Mix with a hand-held blender to obtain a liquid strawberry purée.

10

Strain the purée through a fine sieve to obtain a fine strawberry coulis.

11

Peel the bananas. Cut into rounds. Add the remaining cream and sugar syrup and juice from 1/2 a lemon. Blend until smooth to obtain a banana purée.

12

Run a knife around the mousses to remove from the rings or ramekins. Unmold and serve with the strawberry coulis and banana purée. Decorate with the mint.

CREPES STUFFED
WITH
CHESTNUTS

SERVES : 6

PREPARATION TIME : 30 Minutes
COOKING TIME : 35 Minutes

This recipe uses canned chestnuts, which are available year-round. Classic crepes are filled with a pastry cream and the canned chestnuts and served cold with a raspberry, or other red fruit, purée.

INGREDIENTS

- ☐ 2 cups all-purpose flour
- ☐ 2 eggs
- ☐ 3 tbsps sugar
- ☐ 1½ cups milk
- ☐ 2 tbsps butter, melted
- ☐ 3 egg yolks
- ☐ Half a 1lb can chestnuts in syrup
- ☐ 3 tbsps flour
- ☐ 1 cup milk
- ☐ 1 tbsp marasquin (or other flavored liqueur)
- ☐ ¾ cup cane sugar syrup
- ☐ 1 cup raspberries
- ☐ Oil
- ☐ Fresh mint
- ☐ Pinch salt

1 To make the crepe batter, beat together the flour, eggs, sugar and salt.

2 Add the 1½ cups milk gradually, beating continuously. Then whisk in the melted butter. Set aside to rest.

3 Make the pastry cream by beating together the egg yolks with 4 tbsps of the chestnut syrup and 3 tbsps flour.

4 Bring the milk to a boil. Gradually beat in the egg mixture. Mix together thoroughly and return to the pan to cook, stirring constantly.

5 When the mixture comes to a boil, remove from the heat and add the marasquin and 12 of the canned chestnuts, chopped.

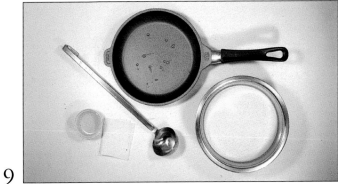

9 Rub a frying pan with a paper towel dipped in oil before cooking each crepe. Add the batter to the pan using a small ladle.

6 Bring the sugar syrup to a boil and add the raspberries. Set aside for 5 minutes.

10 Cook the first side for one minute, then turn and cook the other side for a further minute. Repeat with the rest of the batter.

7 Blend the sugar syrup and raspberries to a smooth purée.

11 Spread each crepe with a little chestnut pastry cream. Fold into four to create small fans.

8 Strain the purée through a fine sieve to obtain a coulis.

12 Serve the crepes hot with the raspberry coulis, a few whole canned chestnuts and bouquets of mint leaves.

PINEAPPLE

AND

MANGO

UPSIDE-DOWN CAKE

SERVES : 6

PREPARATION TIME : 30 to 35 Minutes
COOKING TIME : 50 Minutes

This is a variation on the classic pineapple upside-down cake. Chopped fresh or canned mango and rum are added to the batter. The cake is served with a purée of fresh raspberries.

INGREDIENTS

- [ ] 1½ cups sugar
- [ ] 6 slices pineapple
- [ ] 1 mango
- [ ] 1½ cups all-purpose flour
- [ ] 2 tsps baking powder
- [ ] 5 eggs
- [ ] ½ cup butter
- [ ] 4 tbsps grated coconut
- [ ] 1½ cups canned pineapple juice
- [ ] 1 tbsp coconut liqueur
- [ ] 1 cup raspberry jam
- [ ] 3 tbsps heavy cream
- [ ] Few fresh mint leaves

1 Make a caramel by boiling together ½ of the sugar and 2 tbsps water in a non-stick frying pan.

2 When the caramel is golden brown, pour into the base of a cake pan.

3 Arrange the pineapple slices quickly over the hot caramel. Cool by dipping the base of the pan in cold water.

4 Halve the mango, remove the stone, then make crisscross slashes into the skin and flesh. Turn inside-out, and cut off the squares of flesh.

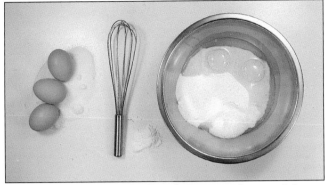

5 In a bowl, mix together the flour, baking powder, remaining 1 cup sugar and the eggs.

6 Add the melted butter and the coconut. Mix together well.

7 Pour the cake batter over the pineapple slices.

8 Arrange the mango cubes over the cake batter, pressing them down into the batter. Bake in a hot oven 400°F for 40 minutes.

9 Turn the cake out onto a cake rack to cool.

10 Mix together half the pineapple juice and the coconut liqueur. Sprinkle over the cake.

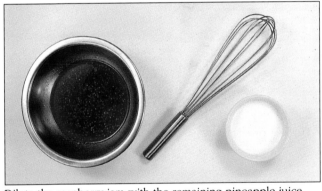

11 Dilute the raspberry jam with the remaining pineapple juice. Beat the cream lightly.

12 When the cake has cooled completely, serve it in slices with the raspberry jam sauce and the cream. Decorate with mint leaf bouquets.

PEAR AND APPLE TART À L'ALSACIENNE

SERVES : 6

PREPARATION TIME : 45 Minutes
COOKING TIME : 30 Minutes

Dishes from Alsace reflect a definite German influence. This one is always a popular dessert. A sweet pastry shell is filled with sliced apples and pears in a rich custard base, then baked in the oven until golden.

INGREDIENTS

- ☐ 2½ cups all-purpose flour
- ☐ ¼ cup water
- ☐ 2 tbsps sugar
- ☐ 1 egg yolk
- ☐ ⅔ cup butter at room temperature
- ☐ 2 apples
- ☐ 2 pears
- ☐ 3 eggs
- ☐ ¾ cup crème fraîche (or heavy cream)
- ☐ ¼ cup milk
- ☐ ⅓ cup sugar
- ☐ 6 tbsps ground almonds
- ☐ Cinnamon
- ☐ 1 tbsp confectioners' sugar
- ☐ 1 tbsp chocolate powder
- ☐ Few leaves fresh mint
- ☐ Salt

1 Place the flour on your work surface, or in a bowl. Make a well in the center and add the water, a pinch of salt, the sugar and egg yolk. Work together with your fingers.

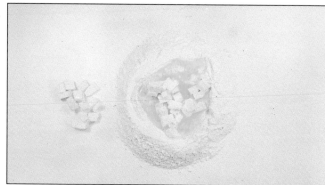

2 Add the butter, in pieces, and mix all the ingredients together thoroughly to form a dough.

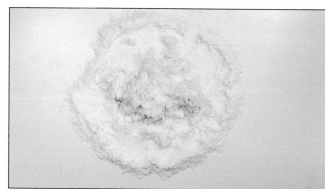

3 Work the pastry dough into a ball, and allow to rest in the refrigerator for 30 minutes.

4 Peel and core the apples. Cut each apple into 8 slices.

5 Peel and core the pears, also cutting each one into 8 slices.

6 To make the custard filling, mix together the eggs, cream, milk, sugar, almonds and cinnamon to taste. Set aside.

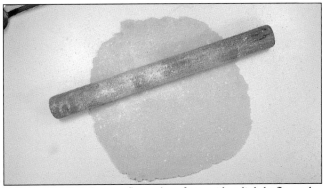

7 Roll out the dough on a floured surface with a lightly floured rolling pin.

8 Line a greased pie pan with the dough. Trim away the excess dough.

9 Make sure the pastry case is sufficiently deep to contain the filling. Prick the bottom of the tart with a fork, and allow to rest in the refrigerator.

10 Arrange the apple and pear slices in the pastry case.

11 Pour the custard filling over the fruit, and bake in a very hot oven 425°F for approximately 25 minutes.

12 Allow to cool in the pan. Remove from the pie pan and dust with confectioners' sugar and chocolate powder. Decorate with the mint leaves.

POULTRY and GAME

MEAT

DESSERTS